TREATING THE TRAUMA SURVIVOR

Treating the Trauma Survivor is a practical guide to assist mental health, healthcare, and social service providers in providing trauma-informed care. This resource provides essential information in order to understand the impact of trauma by summarizing key literature in an easily accessible and user-friendly format. Providers will be able to identify common pitfalls and learn how to avoid retraumatizing survivors during interactions. Based on the authors' extensive experience and interactions with trauma survivors, the book provides a trauma-informed framework and offers practical tools to enhance collaboration with survivors and promote a safer helping environment. Mental health providers in healthcare, community, and addictions settings as well as healthcare providers and community workers will find the framework and the practical suggestions in this book informative and useful.

Carrie Clark is a clinical psychologist. She attained her doctorate from the University of Denver. She completed a postdoctoral fellowship in the Trauma Therapy Program at Women's College Hospital. She is on staff as a clinical psychologist in the Trauma Therapy Program. She specializes in the area of trauma therapy.

Catherine C. Classen is a clinical psychologist with expertise in the treatment of psychological trauma. She is an associate professor in the Department of Psychiatry at the University of Toronto, Senior Scientist and Director of the Women's Mental Health Research Program at Women's College Research Institute, and Academic Leader of the Trauma Therapy Program at Women's College Hospital. She is a past president of the International Society for the Study of Trauma and Dissociation, sits on the editorial board of several trauma journals, and has numerous publications in the area of psychological trauma.

Anne Fourt is an occupational therapist and team coordinator for the Trauma Therapy Program and Women Recovering from Abuse Program at Women's College Hospital. She is an assistant professor in the Occupational Science and Occupational Therapy Department at the University of Toronto and has a cross appointment in the Department of Psychiatry.

Maithili Shetty is a psychiatrist and clinical faculty at the University of British Columbia. She received her medical degree at the University of Western Ontario and completed her residency in psychiatry at the University of Toronto. Dr. Shetty is the Director of Medical Education, Medical Director of the Psychiatric Assessment and Stabilization Unit, and Inpatient Lead for the Department of Psychiatry at St. Paul's Hospital in Vancouver, British Columbia.

TREATING THE TRAUMA SURVIVOR

An Essential Guide to Trauma-Informed Care

Carrie Clark, Catherine C. Classen, Anne Fourt, and Maithili Shetty

Routledge
Taylor & Francis Group

NEW YORK AND LONDON

First published 2015
by Routledge
711 Third Avenue, New York, NY 10017

and by Routledge
27 Church Road, Hove, East Sussex BN3 2FA

Routledge is an imprint of the Taylor & Francis Group, an informa business

Library of Congress Cataloging-in-Publication Data

Clark, Carrie (Clinical psychologist), author.
Treating the trauma survivor : an essential guide to trauma-informed care
/ Carrie Clark, Catherine Classen, Anne Fourt, Maithili Shetty.
    p. ; cm.
  Includes bibliographical references and index.
  I. Classen, Catherine, 1955– author.   II. Fourt, Anne, author.
III. Shetty, Maithili, author.   IV. Title.
  [DNLM: 1. Stress Disorders, Post-Traumatic—therapy. WM 172.5]
  RC552.P67
  616.85'21—dc23
  2014016326

ISBN: 978-1-138-81147-8 (hbk)
ISBN: 978-0-415-81098-2 (pbk)
ISBN: 978-0-203-07062-8 (ebk)

Typeset in Bembo
by Apex CoVantage, LLC

CONTENTS

FIGURES

ABOUT THE AUTHORS

Carrie Clark is a clinical psychologist. She attained her doctorate from the University of Denver. She completed a postdoctoral fellowship in the Trauma Therapy Program at Women's College Hospital. She is on staff as a clinical psychologist in the Trauma Therapy Program. She specializes in the area of trauma therapy.

Catherine C. Classen is a clinical psychologist with expertise in the treatment of psychological trauma. She is an associate professor in the Department of Psychiatry at the University of Toronto, Senior Scientist and Director of the Women's Mental Health Research Program at Women's College Research Institute, and Academic Leader of the Trauma Therapy Program at Women's College Hospital. She is a past president of the International Society for the Study of Trauma and Dissociation, sits on the editorial board of several trauma journals, and has numerous publications in the area of psychological trauma.

Anne Fourt is an occupational therapist, clinician, and team coordinator for the Trauma Therapy Program and Women Recovering from Abuse Program at Women's College Hospital. She is an assistant professor in the Occupational Science and Occupational Therapy Department at the University of Toronto and has a cross appointment in the Department of Psychiatry.

Maithili Shetty is a psychiatrist and clinical faculty at the University of British Columbia. She received her medical degree at the University of Western Ontario and completed her residency in psychiatry at the University of Toronto. Dr. Shetty is the Director of Medical Education, Medical Director of the Psychiatric Assessment and Stabilization Unit, and Inpatient Lead for the Department of Psychiatry at St. Paul's Hospital in Vancouver, British Columbia.

FOREWORD

That complex developmental trauma is prevalent in the lives of many children and has major repercussions across the lifespan is now irrefutable. That complex developmental trauma continues to be denied and unrecognized and that these repercussions continue to be under-acknowledged is also irrefutable. This, despite the ever-accumulating amount of research that substantiates the many ways that such trauma can have a significant impact, from the time of its occurrence forward. The myriad effects of complex trauma have also been identified. In addition to the symptoms associated with the "classic" form of Posttraumatic Stress Disorder (PTSD; i.e., re-experiencing, numbing, altered cognitions and beliefs, and physiological hyper-arousal and hyper-vigilance), the most common aftereffects are developmental, with negative impact on the victim's identity and self-worth, ability to self-regulate, ability to trust and relate to others, spirituality and systems of meaning, and somatic concerns and illness. If this were not enough, since childhood abuse and neglect and other forms of interpersonal victimization have not received public attention until recent times, these effects have long been suppressed, dismissed, and unrecognized. Whether they emerged at the time of the trauma or later in life, they were routinely disconnected from the events and experiences that precipitated them and were left untreated.

Not uncommonly, these untreated effects were disruptive to the individual's development and life trajectory. Victims were left to cope as best they could, in relative isolation and with little support. Some were successful in overcoming the effects and were able to put their lives back on track while others did not fare so well. In many cases, some of the coping mechanisms they used became problems in their own right, including addictions and compulsions, risk-taking, dissociation, anxiety, depression, self-harm, suicidality, and anything else victims could use in the interest of managing what were often onerous memories and symptoms. There were several unfortunate consequences associated with these "secondary elaborations": Victims were often blamed and stigmatized for their problems and seen as weak or pathetic. In the worst cases, they were dismissed as hopeless cases or were subjected to mistreatment or additional abuse, sometimes by the very professionals and organizations responsible for helping them.

As research findings regarding childhood trauma and its effects have proliferated, the range and scope of the problem has become increasingly clear. The impact of childhood trauma has been shown to not only affect the primary victim but to secondarily impact family members and significant others, communities, and society as a whole. It even affects those charged with helping the traumatized. An intergenerational and transgenerational cycle of violence has been identified, driven in large measure by unacknowledged and unprocessed trauma. Trauma, especially of the complex sort that is chronic, cumulative, and progressive in severity and committed by other humans (most often family members and individuals who are otherwise related to the victim in some way), has been highly implicated in this cycle.

Bloom (1995) articulated what she labeled the "germ theory of trauma" to account for this widespread and negative impact of childhood trauma at both the individual and societal level. In her theory, she analogized the discovery of the effects of cumulative developmental trauma and its relation to ongoing societal violence with the discovery of the impact of germs on disease and illness. Until discovered and treated with universal precautions—including public education and the specialized training of medical professionals, improved sanitation, focused medicine, and specialized treatment—germs were the breeding ground and transmission mechanism for disease that infected or killed millions upon millions. In a similar vein, untreated trauma (especially from childhood) is now identified as a mechanism of transmission that needs to be recognized and treated to begin to lessen its negative systemic impact and reverse course.

The Trauma-Informed Care Movement

Trauma-informed care has developed over the course of the past two decades in response to the increased understanding of the role of trauma in the transmission of violence and to the misunderstanding and mistreatment accorded to its victims. It was developed in recognition that the curriculum and training of most professionals has been lacking with regard to attention to trauma and its impact and to provide a corrective. Trauma-informed care refers to a shift in perspective on the part of professionals that recognizes that complex and cumulative trauma is most often the cause of many forms of mental distress. It also has a substantial impact on physical health status, illness, and health maintenance as documented by the findings of Adverse Childhood Events survey of Kaiser Permanente Insurance

Company (ACE; Felitti & Anda, 2010) and in other reviews of the literature on the physical/somatic effects of trauma.

Trauma-informed care has developed as a universal precaution that is recommended for all medical, mental health practitioners, and the many other professionals (i.e., court and criminal justice personnel, police officers, social service workers, etc.) whose caseloads routinely include a high percentage of traumatized individuals. Trauma-informed care involves a stance of respect towards the victim/patient/client and understanding that many of the presenting symptoms may well be secondary elaborations or adaptations developed to deal with the original untreated effects of the trauma. As such, they were survival mechanisms that worked (to a greater or lesser degree) in the short run but that didn't solve the problem and became maladaptive in the long run. TIC begins with a focus on safety and life stabilization, general education about trauma and its common aftereffects, and directed education and skill-building as needed. This largely developmental focus can be followed by trauma-focused treatment methods specifically designed to process and resolve the posttraumatic symptoms.

The trauma-informed approach is based on the understanding that interpersonal victimization, especially when in the context of close relationships, involves betrayal and exploitation. Mistrust of others on the part of the victim is to be expected, as is a relational style that reflects this mistrust and impaired interactions. Helpers strive to be reliable and consistent in ways that earn their clients' trust and know that the quality of the relationship they offer undergirds the healing process. They additionally understand that, as helpers, they will be affected by their exposure to traumatic life experiences and that attention to self-care and personal wellness is an ethical imperative of the work. Additionally, a trauma-informed approach seeks to understand the victim in context (gender, sexual identity and orientation, race, culture, religious, or political group) and to understand how particular contexts may have impacted the trauma, its impact, and idioms of distress. Finally, trauma-informed care provides the foundation and the milieu within which all services (general and trauma-focused) are offered.

This book, with its focus on mental health, medical, and social services, makes a very important contribution to the trauma-informed care literature. Since most trauma survivors are often largely unaware of any possible connection between their past history and their present psychological, physical, and somatic symptoms, the competencies (knowledge, skills, attitudes regarding trauma, and its relation to mental health and medical concerns) on the part of the provider are very meaningful. This book offers a comprehensive overview of complex trauma, its effects, and its ways of presenting in mental health, medical, and social service settings and gives providers essential information in addressing the needs of these individuals. It offers many insights and strategies for management that can assist health and social service providers in providing personalized service to traumatized clients. It is a book that ought to be read and on the bookshelf of all mental health, medical, and social service professionals.

Christine A. Courtois, PhD, ABPP
Psychologist, Private Practice, Washington, DC
Author:

Treating complex traumatic stress disorders in children and adolescents
(2013) (co-edited with Julian Ford)

The treatment of complex trauma: A sequenced, relationship–based approach
(2012) (co-authored with Julian Ford)

Healing the incest wound: Adult survivors in therapy
(2010) (Revised edition)

Treating complex traumatic stress disorders: An evidence-based guide
(co-edited with Julian Ford)

ACKNOWLEDGMENTS

The original manual was made possible through funding from the province of Ontario's Academic Health Sciences Centre Alternative Funding Plan—Innovation Fund, which was awarded to Maithili Shetty at Women's College Hospital, Toronto, Canada. We are grateful to Harjeet Badwall, Deanna Bruno, Ingrid Cologna, Sushma Persaud, and Siraj Waglay for their contributions to the original manual. We thank Liberty Karp for her help with the images. A special word of thanks goes to Agata Drozd for her impeccable editing. We also wish to acknowledge the support and encouragement of Valerie Taylor, the Trauma Therapy Program, the Sexual Assault/Domestic Violence Care Centre, and the entire Women's Mental Health Program, all at Women's College Hospital. Lastly, we thank our clients for allowing us the honour to walk alongside them through some of their journey and trusting us to hear their experiences. It is from this work with clients that we have come to appreciate the necessity of making trauma-informed care a standard, not just in mental health, but in all areas of healthcare and social services.

INTRODUCTION

This book was originally written as an in-house manual for our Urgent Follow-Up Clinic at Women's College Hospital in Toronto, Canada. The Urgent Follow-Up Clinic was designed to meet the clinical needs of those needing urgent but not emergency care. This clinic saw individuals who were assessed in the emergency department and did not require psychiatric admission but who did need urgent care, as routine outpatient services would have involved too long a wait. The treatment focus of the clinic was stabilization of the crisis. This clinic and the approach worked well for certain individuals (i.e., those with a circumscribed crisis in their lives, such as a recent job loss, the onset of psychiatric problems, or the break-up of an intimate relationship). However, there was a subset of individuals for whom this model did not work. Individuals who had chronic and/or complex histories of interpersonal trauma often presented to the emergency department in crisis, but the traditional interventions geared towards stabilization of the crisis were not effective. The imminent crisis was often just one of many struggles occurring in the individual's life.

The providers in the Urgent Follow-Up Clinic realized that effective treatment was needed to address the impact of chronic traumatization and to help survivors manage their longstanding distress. However, they also felt that there were gaps in knowledge among the urgent care providers about chronic trauma and its treatment. Consequently, providers from that clinic partnered with clinicians from the Trauma Therapy Program and the Sexual Assault/Domestic Violence Care Centre, both of which operate at Women's College Hospital, to create a manual on trauma-informed care for the Urgent Follow-Up Clinic. The manual was well received, and with the encouragement of Valerie Taylor, Chief of the Women's Mental Health Program at Women's College Hospital, a subset of the original authors decided to expand the manual and adapt it for providers across healthcare and social service settings.

Many individuals who seek mental health services, physical healthcare services, and social services have a history of complex psychological trauma. Providers working in these fields may or may not know that the individuals with whom they work have a trauma history. When the provider does not know they are working with a survivor of trauma, their understanding of the individual, as well as the interventions and supports offered, may be misdirected or ineffective. This can leave the provider feeling frustrated, confused, ineffectual, and overwhelmed. Meanwhile, the individual seeking help may feel misunderstood, frustrated, hurt, helpless, or even frightened.

Trauma-informed care is an approach that incorporates an understanding of the effects of trauma and violence on an individual and assumes that any individual could have a trauma history. Given the pervasiveness of trauma, this assumption is not only prudent but warranted. Furthermore, this approach is appropriate not only for survivors of trauma, but for all individuals. Trauma-informed care is not a specialized approach; rather, it is the basis for competent work with all.

There are multiple forms of psychological trauma, including war trauma, natural disasters, motor vehicle accidents, child abuse, and cultural and systemic trauma, to name a few. The focus of this book is on interpersonal trauma, especially complex interpersonal trauma. Interpersonal trauma shares many similarities with other forms of trauma, but also has some unique aspects. Specifically, interpersonal trauma occurs in the context of a relationship, often a significant relationship. Consequently, relationships, even those with a professional caregiver (e.g., a therapist, counselor, doctor, or social service provider), can mirror traumatic relational dynamics. Trauma-informed care recognizes this potential and seeks to establish working relationships that are supportive and empowering for the survivor. Our aim is to provide a rudimentary overview of interpersonal trauma, its consequences, and how to work effectively and sensitively with survivors of interpersonal trauma.

Overview of the Book

This book is meant to be a succinct guide to the basics of trauma-informed care. It was written to provide the essentials to a busy provider. The book can be read from start to finish, or chapters can be read in the order of interest or need. Chapter 1 describes what we mean by the term trauma-informed care and provides an explanation of the principles of trauma-informed care. Chapter 2 discusses the most recent developments in trauma-related diagnoses in the *Diagnostic and statistical manual of mental disorders* (DSM-5) and the *World Health Organization International classification of diseases and related health problems* (ICD-11), and it explores the development and utility of the complex PTSD diagnosis as a way of understanding the survivor's experience. Chapter 3 examines the core difficulties associated with complex PTSD, providing the reader with an understanding of the psychology of the survivor. Chapter 4 provides an overview of how providers can build an empowering and collaborative relationship with survivors.

Suggestions about how to respond to disclosures of trauma and violence are discussed in Chapter 5. Chapter 6 describes how to conduct a trauma-informed assessment. Chapter 7 addresses how to respond to safety concerns, including suicidality, self-harm, and current violence, such as domestic violence and sexual assault. Chapter 8 explores various trauma-informed interventions that the provider can use, including psychoeducational material to share with survivors, how to manage dissociation, and the importance of self-care. Chapter 9 describes how to deal with substance use, including assessment, signs and symptoms of withdrawal, withdrawal management, taking a harm-reduction approach, and pharmacotherapy options for substance dependence. Chapter 10 provides a trauma-informed approach to psychiatric medications. Chapter 11 explores the relational dynamics of working with survivors through common transference and countertransference reactions. Lastly, Chapter 12 examines the impact of this work on the provider through vicarious traumatization. One of the co-authors, Shetty, took primary responsibility for Chapters 9 and 10, while Clark, Classen, and Fourt took primary responsibility for the remaining chapters.

Psychoeducational Material

The book contains a number of figures that can be used for psychoeducation with clients. The figures are also provided in the appendix. These figures are not to be used for sale and are only intended for the reader's personal use.

A Note on Language

Our multidisciplinary team of authors (two psychologists, an occupational therapist, and a psychiatrist) aimed to write a succinct book covering the basics of trauma-informed care for providers in various settings. In order to achieve this goal, we had many discussions on the focus and the particular language to use in this book. To begin, we had vigorous conversations about who should be our target audience. Although this book was written by mental health providers and many of the examples are based in mental health settings, we are aware that other healthcare and social service providers play an integral role in the care and support of survivors and can benefit from learning about trauma-informed care. Consequently, when addressing the reader, we aimed to be inclusive and chose to refer to the "provider" as opposed to therapist, clinician, physician, or social service worker.

In addition, we have chosen to refer to the "survivor" as the individual with whom we work. We chose this term over "patient" or "client" for many reasons. A primary reason is that it felt more empowering to label the individuals as survivors of trauma, rather than to use a term that can carry specific context-laden connotations and the related potential power dynamics that are associated with it. Our hope is that in using these terms, professionals working in different roles and in many areas of healthcare and social service will read this book and recognize its relevance to the work they do and that, ultimately, they will be encouraged to incorporate trauma-informed principles into their service delivery.

We have also chosen to eliminate the awkward and cumbersome language of s/he and him/her, and instead use the gender-neutral term of "they." While we recognize this goes against basic grammar rules, there is a current trend towards overriding this rule for the ease of the reader. We appreciate this trend and also prefer how it provides a way to be gender neutral and inclusive of all.

We use the term "trauma" throughout the book and want to be clear about the meaning we intend when we use it. In the trauma literature, this word is often used to refer to either an event or a response to an event. In order to distinguish between these two, we will use the term "trauma" to refer to an event and "traumatization" to refer to the response to the traumatic trauma. Throughout the book, we use "trauma-informed care" and "trauma-informed services" interchangeably.

1

UNDERSTANDING TRAUMA AND TRAUMA-INFORMED CARE

The Basics

What Is Trauma-Informed Care?

A large percentage of the general population has experienced trauma. In the United States the lifetime prevalence rate for exposure to a traumatic event has been estimated at 50–70% of the general population and 90% of public mental health population (Kessler, Sonnega, Bromet, Hughes, & Nelson, 1995). A national prevalence study in Canada found that half of all Canadian women have experienced at least one incident of physical or sexual violence by the age of 16 (Vallaincourt & Marshall, 1993). In Ontario, approximately 31% of males and 21% of females experience childhood physical abuse and 13% of females and 4% of males experience sexual abuse (MacMillan et al., 1997). With a history of trauma, it is far more likely that an individual will come into contact with the healthcare system (McColl et al., 2010; Arnow, 2004; Felitti et al., 1998; Du Mont & White, 2007) and social services (Larkin & Park, 2012). Thus, it is incumbent on mental health, healthcare, and social service providers to be trauma-informed (Bloom & Farragher, 2011).

Trauma-informed services are those that incorporate an understanding of the impact of violence and psychological trauma in the lives of consumers of mental health, healthcare, and social services (Harris & Fallot, 2001b; Bloom & Farragher, 2011). Healthcare and social service professionals who work within a trauma-informed framework understand that traumatic experiences are not rare, but are, in fact, highly prevalent in their communities. Practitioners of trauma-informed care acknowledge the psychological, emotional, physical, and spiritual impact of trauma on the individual. Crucially, within this approach, trauma is also seen as having an effect on the relationships of survivors, including those with health and social service professionals. Acknowledging the impact of trauma requires that the trauma-informed provider adjusts how care is delivered in order to accommodate what the trauma survivor needs—and to deliver it in such a way that the survivor's sense of safety is prioritized.

What Is Trauma?

A traumatic event is one that leaves an individual feeling overwhelmed. The situation is perceived as threatening; it leaves the person feeling out of control or helpless and unable to assimilate or integrate the event. In the *Diagnostic and statistical manual of mental disorders* (5th ed.; DSM-5; American Psychiatric Association, 2013), a traumatic experience is defined as exposure to actual or threatened death, serious injury, or sexual violence, through one (or more) of the following: direct exposure, witnessing, learning about the occurrence of, or experiencing repeated or extreme exposure to traumatic events.

One of the more insidious consequences of experiencing a traumatic event is that the experience overwhelms one's capacity to cope with the trauma. Recognizing this as a key feature of trauma allows for the inclusion of a broad range of events, including child abuse, physical assault, sexual assault, natural and human-made disasters, accidents, combat, being held hostage or in captivity, torture, hate crimes, medical trauma (e.g., becoming conscious during surgery) along with indirect exposure to traumatic events affecting close others.

An individual's *perception* of an event as threatening is a key determinant of his or her traumatization by that event. For example, if a woman is stopped on the street and threatened by a man who says he has a gun in his pocket, traumatization can result regardless of whether or not the man in fact has a gun. If the woman perceives her safety is under threat, it can be traumatic. In short, it is how the individual experiences the event that determines whether or not it is traumatic.

Within a non-trauma-informed approach, traumatic events are conceptualized as rare and discrete events that have predictable consequences for the trauma survivor. Predictable consequences include, for example, the diagnostic criteria that are associated with PTSD: re-experiencing symptoms, hyperarousal, negative changes in mood or cognitions, and avoiding reminders of the trauma. However, this limited definition of traumatic stress has the potential to exclude ongoing forms of violence and other events that might not be life-threatening, but that, nevertheless, significantly impact an individual. Additionally, believing trauma to be a rare event can lead to mental health and healthcare providers' failure to assess for a history of trauma, which is highly problematic given what we know about the frequency with which individuals with histories of trauma utilize the healthcare system. Moreover, by restricting one's understanding of how traumatization manifests in an individual's life to predictable consequences such as the DSM-5 PTSD symptoms, one fails to recognize the plethora of other difficulties to which chronic traumatization often leads. (See Chapter 3 for a discussion of the range of difficulties that can occur among survivors of complex trauma.)

Within a trauma-informed approach, trauma is defined broadly; the prevalence of trauma in the community is acknowledged; and survivors' symptoms are interpreted within the context of their traumatic history and are viewed as adaptations that enable them to cope. Trauma is understood to be diverse in its presentation, complex and broad in its impact on the individual, and oftentimes insidious in the survivor's life. It is also understood that survivors of repeated trauma will often organize their identities around traumatic experiences, as well as basing their fundamental assumptions about others and the world on these experiences (Janoff-Bulman, 1992). This organization around trauma consequently impacts their subsequent choices and life events.

The Survivor

When a non-trauma-informed approach is employed, the focus is on the survivor's presenting symptoms rather than on understanding the context within which those symptoms developed. This approach has the tendency to view problematic behaviour as symptomatic of some deeper pathology. The goal within a non-trauma-informed approach is to reduce or eliminate the trauma survivor's symptoms. However, this focus on simply eliminating problematic behaviour is limited in that it does not recognize that it serves a purpose in the survivor's life. In other words, the underlying function of the behaviour is often overlooked.

When a trauma-informed approach is utilized, symptoms are viewed as coping strategies adopted by the trauma survivor (Courtois & Gold, 2009), and it is understood that these symptoms likely arose within the context of trauma (Harris & Fallot, 2001b). A trauma-informed approach takes an adaptive, rather than a pathologizing, view of symptoms. Consequently, symptoms are understood to be creative attempts to cope with overwhelming distress. These behaviours are seen as an attempt to cope with an untenable situation in the context of a history of trauma, rather than being seen as symptoms of some larger underlying disturbance (Briere, 1992). For example, when using the non-trauma-informed approach, self-harm may be viewed as a dysfunctional, attention-seeking behaviour. In contrast, utilizing the trauma-informed approach is more likely to lead to an assessment of self-harm as an individual's attempt to self-regulate overwhelming affect. In fact, one of the hallmark symptoms of survivors of trauma is a difficulty with self-regulation (i.e., regulating emotions, behaviour, cognitions, bodily function; van der Kolk, 1996; 2005). Many of the behaviours exhibited by trauma survivors can be understood as helping to regulate dysregulated affect. These behaviours can be so effective in achieving this regulation that they become patterned ways of coping, and while these coping strategies often occur at a cost to the individual (for example, substance abuse, self-harm, dissociation), they also tend to be reliable and effective ways of coping and are, thus, not easily eliminated.

The concept of complex PTSD has been developed to describe the difficulties of individuals who have experienced ongoing traumatization (Herman, 1992;

van der Kolk, Roth, Pelcovitz, & Mandel, 1993). The concept outlines seven dimensions of functioning that can be affected by repeated trauma:

1. Affect regulation (e.g., being chronically distressed or in a state of hyper-arousal or hypoarousal; engaging in risky behaviours);
2. Biological self-regulation (e.g., somatization);
3. Consciousness (e.g., dissociation);
4. Self-perception (e.g., feelings of self-hate or self-blame);
5. Perception of the perpetrator (e.g. idealizing the abuser);
6. Relations with others (e.g., difficulty trusting or feeling overly dependent or needy); and
7. Systems of meaning (e.g., feeling hopeless about the future).

This concept outlines the ways in which trauma can impact and shape one's identity and can affect the various areas of functioning. With a more complete picture of the impact of chronic trauma, the mental health, healthcare, and social service provider will be in a better position to provide trauma-informed care.

The Role of Services

The relationship between trauma and health services can be examined by looking at the rates of seeking various health services. There is a strong relationship between a history of trauma and use of health services—use by survivors of trauma is much higher than use by non-survivors. Explanations for this relationship include both psychiatric and medical comorbidity—some survivors access health services to treat depression or anxiety, for example, while others present with medical concerns (e.g., diabetes, heart disease, fibromyalgia; Kessler et al., 1995; Deykin et al., 2001). Consequently, individuals with trauma histories frequently access healthcare. For example, one study found that 37% of patients who visited emergency departments had histories of emotional or physical abuse, while 14% reported abuse in the previous year (Dearwater et al., 1998). Survivors of childhood abuse also make more emergency room visits (Arnow, Hart, Hayward, Dea, & Taylor, 2000; Arnow et al., 1999) and have more hospitalizations (McCauley et al., 1997). These findings suggest that inquiring about a history of trauma should be standard procedure.

Survivors often present for medical and mental health reasons that are not related to their trauma histories in any obvious way. In fact, more often than not, individuals with histories of trauma present with issues that are related to some current source of distress and not to their history of trauma. This underscores the need for an understanding of the role and impact of a history of trauma on an individual's current functioning.

Non-trauma-informed and trauma-informed approaches can also be contrasted with regard to how the goals of services are differentially defined within each approach. Within the non-trauma-informed understanding of services, the goal is often defined as a re-establishment of baseline functioning. As a result, many services are crisis-oriented, with the goal being stabilization (Harris & Fallot, 2001b). A trauma-informed service would focus on stabilization, but would also include the goal of empowering the individual. Consequently, instead of focusing solely on symptom management, services can be geared towards skill-building (Harris & Fallot, 2001b). In addition to understanding symptoms as adaptations, in a trauma-informed approach, the survivor's strengths and resources are incorporated into the understanding of them as a survivor. This approach is especially important in a crisis clinic, as an empowerment model that focuses on the acquisition of skills and building on survivors' strengths may, ultimately, support them through future challenges in life.

The Therapeutic Relationship

Non-trauma-informed service relationships are hierarchical in nature, positioning the provider as the holder of expert knowledge and the survivor as the passive recipient of this knowledge. These relationships have the effect of taking power and agency away from the survivor. In addition, the expert initiates an intervention aimed at managing the symptoms or providing stabilization (Freeman, 2001).

Within a trauma-informed approach, there is recognition of the implications of power in trauma survivors' relationships. Trauma survivors have often had power taken from them in their relationships. To counteract this, a trauma-informed approach strives to work collaboratively with survivors, inviting them to participate in treatment planning and encouraging the empowerment of the individual. A trauma-informed relationship with a survivor will emphasize ensuring the survivor's sense of safety, trust, choice, collaboration, and empowerment (Fallot, 2008). Ultimately, the goal of developing a trauma-informed relationship is to facilitate growth and change (Freeman, 2001). Providers may facilitate this by focusing on the strengths of the survivor and intervening in a way that increases the individual's knowledge, understanding, and skill repertoire.

The Cost of Non-Trauma-Informed Care

There is a significant cost to not adopting trauma-informed care as a standard practice. There is considerable evidence to suggest that trauma survivors often seek help from medical providers (Felitti et al., 1998; Courtois & Gold, 2009). Thus, healthcare professions need to be knowledgeable about trauma and its consequences. Many providers lack adequate knowledge and skill related to trauma, which leaves survivors vulnerable to inadequate treatment (Gold, 2000). Risks include unnecessary hospitalizations, inappropriate treatment or prescribing of medications, inadvertent retraumatization, and inability to make appropriate referrals. A "second injury" (Symonds, 1975) can result when a survivor's primary trauma is exacerbated by an insensitive helper's response. Inquiring about trauma leads to recognizing trauma, and recognizing trauma is an important first step in providing trauma-informed care.

In the chapters that follow, we hope to provide mental health, healthcare, and social service providers with the rudimentary knowledge they need to work sensitively and effectively with trauma survivors.

Questions to Think About

1. Given the frequency of traumatic events in people's lives, how many people with whom you work, on average, do you think have experienced trauma?
2. In order to provide individuals with optimum healthcare and/or social services, why is it important to understand that they may have been traumatized?
3. Why do providers need to pay attention to power dynamics in helping relationships?
4. What is the cost of non-trauma-informed care for those who are traumatized and for the broader health system?
5. How might a trauma-informed approach change one's attitude towards survivors' symptoms?

2

TRAUMA AND THE DSM

Overview

While trauma has always been an inescapable fact of human existence, it was not until 1980 that a diagnostic category to reflect the impact of traumatization was introduced to the *Diagnostic and statistical manual of mental disorders* (DSM). Before the introduction of posttraumatic stress disorder (PTSD), we spoke of hysteria, shell shock, gross stress reaction, transient situational disturbance, "rape trauma syndrome" (Burgess & Holmstrom, 1974), and "battered woman syndrome" (Walker, 1977/78). Few of these labels, however, were associated with any operational definition (Lamprecht & Sack, 2002). The diagnosis of PTSD was the first to incorporate an etiological agent as a necessary component of the diagnosis. In other words, a traumatic stressor is required for the diagnosis to be made. Up until the most recent edition of the DSM, PTSD was categorized as an anxiety disorder. There have been some important changes with regard to trauma-related diagnoses in the current version, DSM-5 (American Psychiatric Association, 2013). The diagnoses most relevant to trauma include PTSD, acute stress disorder, and the dissociative disorders.

Individuals seen in both medical and community settings often have a diagnosis of PTSD or another diagnosis related to trauma. Thus, it is important for practitioners to understand these diagnoses. In addition, it is important to understand what the diagnoses capture as well as what they miss.

The DSM-5

The DSM-5 introduced trauma and stress-related disorders as a new diagnostic category. The following diagnoses are included within this category: reactive attachment disorder, disinhibited social engagement disorder, PTSD, acute stress disorder, and adjustment disorders. For each of these disorders, exposure to a traumatic or stressful event is listed as a diagnostic criterion. This category was listed adjacent to the anxiety disorders, obsessive-compulsive disorders, and dissociative disorders in an effort to reflect the close relationships between these diagnoses (DSM-5, American Psychiatric Association, 2013). Other disorders often diagnosed in those who have experienced trauma include depressive disorders, anxiety disorders, eating disorders, substance-related and addictive disorders, dissociative disorders, and somatic symptom disorders.

The central focus of this chapter is the formulation of the diagnosis of PTSD in the DSM, as this is the diagnosis most frequently given to those who have experienced trauma. However, we will also address acute stress disorder, dissociative identity disorder, and dissociative disorder not otherwise specified, as these are also highly relevant trauma-related diagnoses.

Posttraumatic Stress Disorder

History of PTSD.   Posttraumatic stress disorder was initially introduced in the DSM-III, published in 1980. The impetus for this diagnosis was the growing recognition of the psychological impact of war-time trauma on returning soldiers. While the impact of trauma on mental health had been recognized by mental health clinicians for over a century, it was not until the return of veterans from the Vietnam War that there was a push for an operationalized definition, resulting in the formulation of PTSD. This diagnosis legitimized the observation that extremely traumatic events could produce chronic clinical sequelae in otherwise nonsymptomatic individuals (Yehuda & McFarlane, 1995). Up until this point, stress was understood as initiating or exacerbating only *preexisting* vulnerabilities, and had not been conceptualized as also potentially causing chronic symptom development in relatively normal individuals (Yehuda & McFarlane, 1995).

In the fourth edition of the DSM (4th ed., text rev.; DSM-IV-TR; American Psychiatric Association, 2000), the PTSD diagnosis described the symptomatic developments that followed exposure to a traumatic event. A triad of PTSD symptoms was listed, including re-experiencing (e.g., flashbacks and nightmares), numbing and avoidance of reminders of the trauma (e.g., avoiding thoughts and feelings associated with trauma, and feeling detached from others or oneself), and increased arousal (e.g., hypervigilance and difficulty falling asleep).

PTSD and the DSM-5.   The DSM-5 was published in June of 2013. (American Psychiatric Association) and includes some important changes to the PTSD diagnostic criteria. First, the DSM-5 is more specific about how a traumatic event can be experienced: directly, indirectly, or witnessed. Secondly, the subjective reaction of experiencing "intense fear, helplessness, or horror" (DSM-IV-TR, American Psychiatric Association, 2000) has been removed. Thirdly, instead of three symptom clusters (re-experiencing, avoidance/numbing, and arousal), there are four symptom clusters: re-experiencing, avoidance, negative alterations in cognitions and mood, and arousal. Lastly, the DSM-5 includes two new dissociative subtypes and addresses children who are six years old or younger.

Posttraumatic Stress Disorder

Diagnostic Criteria 309.81 (F43.10)

Note: The following criteria apply to adults, adolescents, and children older than six years. [For children six years or younger, see corresponding criteria.]

A. Exposure to actual or threatened death, serious injury, or sexual violation in one (or more) of the following ways:
1. Directly experiencing the traumatic event(s).
2. Witnessing, in person, the event(s) as it occurred to others.
3. Learning that the event(s) occurred to a close family member or close friend. **Note:** In cases of actual or threatened death of a family member or friend, the event(s) must have been violent or accidental.
4. Experiencing repeated or extreme exposure to aversive details of the traumatic event(s) (e.g., first responders collecting human remains, police officers repeatedly exposed to details of child abuse).
Note: Criterion A4 does not apply to exposure through electronic media, television, movies or pictures, unless this exposure is work related.

B. Presence of one (or more) of the following intrusion symptoms associated with traumatic events), beginning after the traumatic event(s) occurred:
1. Recurrent, involuntary, and intrusive distressing memories of the traumatic event(s).
Note: In children, repetitive play may occur in which themes or aspects of the traumatic event(s) are expressed.
2. Recurrent distressing dreams in which the content and/or affect of the dream are related to the event(s).
Note: in children, there may be frightening dreams without recognizable content.
3. Dissociative reactions (e.g., flashbacks) in which the individual feels or acts as if the traumatic event(s) were recurring. (Such reactions may occur on a continuum, with the most extreme expression being a complete loss of awareness of present surroundings.)
Note: In children, trauma-specific reenactments may occur in play.
4. Intense or prolonged psychological distress or marked physiological reactions in response to internal or external cues that symbolize or resemble an aspect of the traumatic event(s).
5. Marked physiological reactions to internal or external cues that symbolize or resemble an aspect of the traumatic event(s).

C. Persistent avoidance of stimuli associated with the traumatic events(s), beginning after the traumatic event(s) occurred, as evidenced by one or both of the following:
6. Avoidance of or efforts to avoid distressing memories, thoughts, or feelings about or closely associated with the traumatic event(s).
7. Avoidance of or efforts to avoid external reminders (people, places, conversations activities, objects, situations) that arouse distressing memories, thoughts or feelings about or closely associated with the traumatic event(s).

FIGURE 2.1 Posttraumatic stress disorder diagnostic criteria (DSM-5; American Psychiatric Association, 2013).

D. Negative alterations in cognitions and mood associated with the traumatic event(s), beginning or worsening after the traumatic event(s) occurred, as evidenced by two (or more) of the following:
   1. Inability to remember an important aspect of the traumatic event(s) (typically due to dissociative amnesia and not to other factors such as head injury, alcohol, or drugs).
   2. Persistent and exaggerated negative beliefs or expectations about oneself, others, or the world (e.g., "I am bad," "No one can be trusted," "The world is completely dangerous," "My whole nervous system is permanently ruined").
   3. Persistent, distorted cognitions about the cause or consequences of the traumatic event(s) that lead the individual to blame himself/herself or others.
   4. Persistent negative emotional state (e.g., fear, horror, anger, guilt, or shame).
   5. Markedly diminished interest or participation in significant activities.
   6. Feelings of detachment or estrangement from others.
   7. Persistent inability to experience positive emotions (e.g., inability to experience happiness, satisfaction, or loving feelings).

E. Marked alterations in arousal and reactivity associated with the traumatic event(s) beginning or worsening after the traumatic event(s) occurred, as evidenced by two (or more) of the following:
   1. Irritable behaviour and angry outbursts (with little or no provocation), typically expressed as verbal or physical aggression toward people or objects.
   2. Reckless or self-destructive behaviour
   3. Hypervigilance.
   4. Exaggerated startle response.
   5. Problems with concentration.
   6. Sleep disturbance (e.g., difficulty falling or staying sleep, restless sleep).

F. Duration of the disturbance (Criterion B, C, D, and E) is more than one month.
G. The disturbance causes clinically significant distress or impairment in the social, occupational or other important areas of functioning.
H. The disturbance is not attributable to the physiological effect of a substance (e.g., medication, alcohol) or another medical condition.

Specify whether:
With dissociative symptoms: The individual's symptoms meet the criteria for post-traumatic stress disorder, and in addition, in response to the stressor, the individual experiences persistent or recurrent symptoms of either of the following:
1. **Depersonalization:** Persistent or recurrent experiences of feeling detached from, and as if one were an outside observer of, one's mental processes or body (e.g., feeling as though one were in a dream; feeling a sense of unreality of self or body or of time moving slowly).
2. **Derealization:** Persistent or recurrent experiences of unreality of surroundings (e.g., the world around the individual is experienced as unreal, dreamlike, distant, or distorted).

Note: To use this subtype, the dissociative symptoms must not be attributable to the physiological effect of a substance (e.g., blackouts, behaviour during alcohol intoxication) or another medical condition (e.g., complex partial seizures).

Specify if:
With delayed expression: If the full diagnostic criteria are not met until at least six months after the event (although the onset and expression of some symptoms may be immediate).

FIGURE 2.1 Continued

Acute Stress Disorder

History of acute stress disorder.   With the introduction of PTSD in the third edition of the DSM (3rd ed.; DSM–III; American Psychiatric Association, 1980), a diagnostic gap was also introduced: At least four weeks must have passed since the traumatic event in order for the person to receive a PTSD diagnosis. This meant that immediately following a trauma, an individual who was symptomatic would not have been able to receive an appropriate diagnosis until at least four weeks after the traumatic event had occurred. This problem was recognized and corrected with the introduction of acute stress disorder in the DSM-IV. This diagnosis captures those who are symptomatic within the first four weeks following a traumatic experience.

Acute stress disorder and the DSM-5.   In the DSM-5, important changes were made to the diagnostic criteria of acute stress disorder. As with the changes for PTSD, the diagnosis specifies that the trauma can be experienced either directly, indirectly, or witnessed. Also mirroring the revised PTSD definition was the removal of the requirement of a subjective reaction of "intense fear, helplessness, or horror." The most significant change from the DSM-IV-TR to the DSM-5 was the reduced emphasis on dissociative symptoms. The DSM-IV-TR emphasized dissociative symptoms over avoidance and hyperarousal symptoms. The DSM-5 diagnostic criteria now reflect a more heterogeneous presentation, allowing for *any* 9 of 14 symptoms listed in order to meet criteria for acute stress disorder.

Acute Stress Disorder

Diagnostic Criteria 308.3 (F43.0)

A.   Exposure to actual or threatened death, serious injury, or sexual violation in one (or more) of the following ways:
   1.   Directly experiencing the traumatic event(s).
   2.   Witnessing, in person, the event(s) as it occurred to others.
   3.   Learning that the event(s) occurred to a close family member or close friend.
      Note: In cases of actual or threatened death of a family member or friend, the event(s) must have been violent or accidental.
   4.   Experiencing repeated or extreme exposure to aversive details of the traumatic event(s) (e.g., first responders collecting human remains, police officers repeatedly exposed to details of child abuse).
      Note: This does not apply to exposure through electronic media, television, movies or pictures, unless this exposure is work related.

B.   Presence of nine (or more) of the following symptoms from any of the five categories of intrusion, negative mood, dissociation, avoidance, and arousal, beginning or worsening after the traumatic event(s) occurred:

FIGURE 2.2 Acute stress disorder diagnostic criteria (DSM-5; American Psychiatric Association, 2013).

Intrusion Symptoms

1. Recurrent, involuntary, and intrusive distressing memories of the traumatic event(s).
   Note: In children, repetitive play may occur in which themes or aspects of the traumatic event(s) are expressed.
2. Recurrent distressing dreams in which the content and/or affect of the dream are related to the event(s).
   Note: in children, there may be frightening dreams without recognizable content.
3. Dissociative reactions (e.g., flashbacks) in which the individual feels or acts as if the traumatic event(s) were recurring. (Such reactions may occur on a continuum, with the most extreme expression being a complete loss of awareness of present surroundings.)
   Note: In children, trauma-specific reenactments may occur in play.
4. Intense or prolonged psychological distress or marked physiological reactions in response to internal or external cues that symbolize or resemble an aspect of the traumatic event(s).

Negative Mood

5. Persistent inability to experience positive emotions (e.g., inability to experience happiness, satisfaction, or loving feelings).

Dissociative Symptoms

6. An altered sense of the reality of one's surroundings or oneself (e.g., seeing oneself from another perspective, being in a daze, time slowing).
7. Inability to remember an important aspect of the traumatic event(s) (typically due to dissociative amnesia and not to other factors such as head injury, alcohol, or drugs).

Avoidance Symptoms

8. Efforts to avoid distressing memories, thoughts, or feelings about or closely associated with the traumatic event(s).
9. Efforts to avoid external reminders (people, places, conversations activities, objects, situations) that arouse distressing memories, thoughts or feelings about or closely associated with the traumatic event(s).

Arousal Symptoms

10. Sleep disturbance (e.g., difficulty falling or staying sleep, restless sleep).
11. Irritable behaviour and angry outbursts (with little or no provocation), typically expressed as verbal or physical aggression toward people or objects.
12. Hypervigilance.
13. Problems with concentration.
14. Exaggerated startle response.

C. Duration of the disturbance (Symptoms in Criterion B) is three days to one month after trauma exposure.
   Note: Symptoms typically begin immediately after the trauma, but persistence for at least three days and up to a month is needed to meet disorder criteria.

D. The disturbance causes clinically significant distress or impairment in social, occupational, or other important areas of functioning.

E. The disturbance is not attributable to the physiological effects of a substance (e.g., medication or alcohol) or another medical condition (e.g., mild traumatic brain injury) and is not better explained by brief psychotic disorder.

FIGURE 2.2 Continued

Dissociative Disorders

The DSM-5 includes a category for Dissociative Disorders. Within this category are dissociative identity disorder (DID), dissociative amnesia, depersonalization/ derealization disorder, other specified dissociation disorder, and unspecified disso- ciative disorder. This category has been placed next to the trauma and stress-related disorders to acknowledge that dissociative disorders are frequently experienced in the aftermath of trauma and are, thus, closely related to the trauma disorders (DSM-5; American Psychiatric Association, 2013). The physiological effects of a substance-related or medical condition should be ruled out for each of these disorders.

Although there is controversy regarding the existence of DID, including whether or not it is an iatrogenic disorder, most clinicians who work with chronic traumatization have come across someone who has DID, whether or not the cli- nician recognizes it. Dissociation is a common response to severe and chronic trauma, particularly if the trauma was experienced in childhood. With repeated traumatization, the dissociative defense of compartmentalizing the traumatic experience becomes entrenched and further compartmentalization is required in order to allow the individual to function and maintain critical relationships. This fragmenting or compartmentalization of the psyche results in DID for the most severely traumatized individuals.

Dissociative identity disorder. For a person to be diagnosed with DID, the DSM-5 requires that the individual exhibit at least two distinct personality states that are either observed by others or reported by the individual themselves. Unlike the requirements of the DSM-IV, within the new definition, it is not necessary for the clinician to witness the different personality states; it is enough for the survivor to describe them. The compartmentalization of identity results in different personality states, each of which is associated with its own unique sense of self and agency, affect, cognition, memory, consciousness, perception, behaviour, and somatic experience. The survivor must also report gaps in memory. It should be noted that individuals with DID can be adept at hiding their condition, especially from those with whom they have not established trust.

Dissociative amnesia. Dissociative amnesia is a diagnosis that is appropriate for individuals who cannot recall important autobiographical information and is more than ordinary forgetting. Dissociative amnesia usually occurs after a traumatic or stressful experience, and it should cause significant distress or impairment in the individual's functioning.

Depersonalization/derealization. Depersonalization/derealization disorder involves the persistent or repeated experience of either depersonalization or derealization. Depersonalization is when an individual's experience of themselves

Dissociative Identity Disorder

Diagnostic Criteria 300.14 (F44.81)

A. Disruption of identity characterized by two or more distinct personality states, which may be described in some cultures as an experience of possession. The disruption in identity involves marked discontinuity in sense of self and sense of agency, accompanied by related alterations in affect, behaviour, consciousness, memory, perception, cognition, and/or sensory-motor functioning. These signs and symptoms may be observed by others or reported by the individual.

B. Recurrent gaps in the recall of everyday events, important personal information, and/or traumatic events that are inconsistent with ordinary forgetting.

C. The symptoms cause clinically significant distress or impairment in social, occupational, or other important areas of functioning.

D. The disturbance is not a normal part of a broadly accepted cultural or religious practice.
Note: In children, the symptoms are not better explained by imaginary playmates or other fantasy play.

E. The symptoms are not attributable to the physiological effects of a substance (e.g., blackouts or chaotic behaviour during alcohol intoxication) or another medical condition (e.g., complex partial seizures).

FIGURE 2.3 Dissociative identity disorder diagnostic criteria (DSM-5; American Psychiatric Association, 2013).

feels unreal, detached, or as if they are an outside observer of their own experience. Derealization, on the other hand, is the experience of a sense of unreality or detachment regarding one's surroundings. This disorder is not necessarily caused by trauma. It is also a disorder that is most likely to start in childhood or adolescence.

Diagnosing the Effects of Complex Trauma

Complex trauma is interpersonal trauma that occurs repeatedly over a long period of time and is profoundly threatening to the person's life or sense of self. It is not uncommon for survivors with a history of chronic trauma to receive a number of psychiatric diagnoses in an attempt to capture the full spectrum of their difficulties. This is especially true for those whose trauma began in childhood. Consequently, survivors may be given a number of diagnoses, including PTSD, eating disorders, substance use disorders, borderline personality disorder, bipolar disorder, somatoform disorder, dissociative disorders, etc. Unfortunately, despite the many available diagnoses, none of these alone or in any combination adequately capture the difficulties of a survivor of complex trauma.

What started with anecdotal reports and later substantiated by research, the psychological disturbances of those who survived ongoing trauma (as opposed to single-incident trauma) were not fully accounted for by the PTSD diagnosis. The diagnosis of PTSD, as defined by the DSM, did not adequately reflect the influence of prolonged abuse, disrupted attachment, and terror on an individual.

Complex PTSD

In the early 1990s, leaders in the trauma field explored the effects of chronic interpersonal trauma, compared to single-incident trauma, in an attempt to develop a diagnostic framework that would more accurately account for the difficulties faced by survivors of repeated childhood trauma. The constellation of symptoms that these investigators identified has been referred to as complex PTSD (CPTSD), or disorders of extreme stress not otherwise specified (DESNOS; Herman, 1992; Pelcovitz et al., 1997). The concept of CPTSD (or DESNOS) describes seven areas of self-regulatory difficulties, involving alterations in:

1. Affect and impulse regulation (e.g., being chronically distressed or in a state of hyperarousal or hypoarousal; engaging in risky behaviours).
2. Biological self-regulation (e.g., somatic symptoms that cannot be medically explained).
3. Attention or consciousness (e.g., dissociation).
4. Perceptions of the perpetrator (e.g., idealizing the abuser).
5. Self-perception (e.g., feelings of self-hate or self-blame).
6. Relationships (e.g., difficulty trusting others or feeling overly dependent or needy).
7. Systems of meaning or sustaining beliefs (e.g., feeling hopeless about the future).

The DSM and Complex PTSD

In the DSM-IV-TR, the "associated features and disorders" section listed symptoms often exhibited by individuals who have experienced interpersonal violence, such as childhood sexual or physical abuse, intimate partner violence, and being held hostage or tortured. Symptoms listed under "associated features" included "impaired affect modulation; self-destructive and impulsive behaviour; dissociative symptoms; somatic complaints; feelings of ineffectiveness; shame, despair, or hopelessness; feeling permanently damaged; a loss of previously sustained beliefs; hostility; social withdrawal; feeling constantly threatened; impaired relationships with others; or a change from the individual's previous personality characteristics" (American Psychiatric Association, 2000, p. 465). However, as associated features, these symptoms were not required to receive the diagnosis of PTSD.

The DSM-5 has attempted to account for some of the difficulties experienced by those who have been chronically traumatized by expanding the symptoms included in the PTSD diagnosis. A new symptom cluster—negative alternations in cognitions and mood—was added, and new symptoms were included. These new symptoms are related to dysregulation and negative self-concept, including negative beliefs about oneself, others, or the world; distorted thinking about the traumatic event leading to self-blame or blaming others; and negative emotions, such as guilt, or shame. As well, included under arousal and reactivity is reckless or self-destructive behaviours. Along with the expanded symptom list, the DSM-5 added a new subtype "with dissociative symptoms." This subtype is applied when an individual meets criteria for PTSD, and they experience either depersonalization symptoms (e.g., persistent feeling of being detached from one's mental processes or body) or derealization (e.g., persistent feeling of the world not being real). With these additions the DSM-5 PTSD does a better job of capturing some of the symptoms associated with complex PTSD.

Furthermore, under the PTSD differential diagnosis section in the DSM-5, the issue of personality disorders is addressed. It states that interpersonal difficulties which arise or are accentuated as a result of trauma are to be considered an indication of PTSD. This issue was not addressed in the DSM-IV-TR, and is thus a welcome addition in the DSM-5.

Does the DSM-5 capture the effects of chronic trauma? It will take time to assess whether this revision and expansion of the PTSD diagnosis adequately captures the symptoms and struggles experienced by those who have been chronically traumatized. However, an important gap in the diagnostic criteria is that it fails to address the interpersonal difficulties that survivors of chronic trauma tend to experience, even though interpersonal problems are acknowledged as an associated feature.

ICD-11 and Complex PTSD

The upcoming, 11th version of the *World Health Organization International classification of diseases and related health problems* (ICD), scheduled for release in 2015, appears to be taking a different approach to addressing the problem of simple versus complex PTSD (Cloitre, Garvert, Brewin, Bryant, & Maercker, 2013).

While it appears that the DSM-5 has attempted to cover both PTSD and complex PTSD under the diagnosis of PTSD, the proposal for the ICD-11 is to distinguish between the two. The ICD-11 proposal states that PTSD and complex PTSD are "sibling disorders," meaning they are both traumatic stress disorders. However, regardless of the nature of the actual traumatic stressor (single event versus prolonged and pervasive events, for example), the diagnosis is determined by an individual's symptom profile (Cloitre et al., 2013). Unlike the DSM-5, the ICD-11 proposal has attempted to simplify the PTSD diagnosis by including only three core elements, each of which is associated with three symptoms:

1. Re-experiencing: for example, has dreams/nightmares, relives the trauma.
2. Avoidance: for example, avoids thoughts/feelings, activities.
3. A sense of threat: for example, is overly alert, easily startled.

The diagnosis for complex PTSD is characterized by the core symptoms of PTSD plus three additional elements as follows:

1. Impairments in affective regulation: for example, uncontrollable anger, feelings easily hurt.
2. Negative self-concept: for example, feelings of worthlessness, guilt.
3. Impaired relational functioning: for example, cannot feel close to another, distant from others.

The ICD-11 proposal offers a simplified set of diagnostic criteria compared to the DSM-5. In addition, unlike the PTSD criteria in the DSM-5, the interpersonal difficulties experienced by survivors of complex trauma are addressed. By creating two distinct diagnostic categories, PTSD and CPTSD, a more precise conceptualization of the effects of a range of traumatic experiences is made possible and, ideally, this will lead to appropriate treatment plans for clients depending upon their diagnosis. These two diagnostic categories will also facilitate research to understand and address the specific treatment needs of simple versus complex PTSD.

The Importance of a Trauma-Informed Understanding of Complex Trauma

A trauma-informed approach employs a more holistic and comprehensive understanding of survivors' characteristic difficulties and adaptations to chronic trauma. To the trauma-*uninformed*, the survivor of complex trauma may be seen as having multiple, distinct problems that need separate attention and treatment. Without a broader conceptual framework for understanding the effect of complex trauma, survivors often receive multiple diagnoses along with misdirected and less helpful treatment. The need for CPTSD arose because the PTSD diagnosis did not fully address the emotional dysregulation, depression, anxiety, self-hatred, dissociation, substance abuse, self-destructive and risk-taking behaviours, revictimization, problems with interpersonal and intimate relationships, and medical and somatic complaints often experienced by those who have been chronically abused (Courtois, 2004). Moreover, clinicians note that it is these difficulties that are hardest to treat (Courtois, 2004). An appreciation of the complicated nature of CPTSD allows us to better understand survivors and thus provide them with better care. Consequently, the concept of CPTSD may be useful to the provider in thinking about survivors of chronic trauma. CPTSD is explored more extensively in Chapter 3: "Understanding the Complex Picture of Complex Trauma."

Questions to Think About

Juliette is referred for therapy after a recent suicide attempt. The referral form describes how she made several cuts on the inside of her thighs, including one that was particularly deep and required medical attention. At the hospital, she received 28 stitches for her injuries. She reports using cocaine and marijuana on a regular basis. She is currently unemployed, and has struggled to keep a job for longer than six months. She reports a history of restrictive eating, which she continues to struggle with on occasion. She has been in therapy many times, but either finds therapists don't understand her, or initially appear to, but then sooner or later they let her down or reject her. She struggles with lasting friendships, and recently had to move out of an apartment she shared with a friend because they got into an argument. Juliette wonders if it is better for her to live on her own, because she feels she is toxic to all people and situations. Over the course of the assessment, Juliette discloses a trauma history. In discussing her previous diagnoses, Juliette reports she has received multiple diagnoses, but has never been previously diagnosed with PTSD or Complex PTSD.

1.   Reflect on how you might respond if Juliette asked you why no one else has ever recognized that trauma could account for some of her lifelong difficulties.
2.   How can the DSM-5 be useful to providers and survivors who do not meet criteria for a diagnosis?
3.   How might you respond to a survivor who experiences receiving a diagnosis as being "put in a box, dehumanized, and disempowered"?
4.   Considering what you have learned about the impact of trauma on survivors, how might you respond to a survivor who feels that they are hopeless and are doomed to struggle with these severe effects of trauma forever?

3

UNDERSTANDING THE COMPLEX PICTURE OF COMPLEX TRAUMA

This chapter provides an overview of the difficulties faced by survivors of complex trauma.

What Is Complex Trauma?

Complex trauma is typically defined as trauma that has occurred as a result of chronic trauma; that is, it involves a traumatic stressor that occurred over time, was repetitive or included multiple incidents, and was usually of an interpersonal nature (Courtois & Ford, 2013). Often, the trauma begins in early life and involves the child's caregiving system. It may include prolonged physical, emotional, and sexual abuse, as well as profound neglect, all of which have a major developmental impact that persists into adulthood. It has also been suggested that complex trauma can develop as a result of an extreme stressor that is especially threatening or horrific (Courtois, 2004).

Developmental Trauma

Complex trauma has a profound impact on the individual. If it occurs in childhood, it is often referred to as developmental trauma. Complex trauma in childhood interrupts normal development, leading to changes in the brain (Bremner, Vermetten, & Lanius, 2010). Overwhelming physical and emotional trauma will elicit survival responses from the brain and, if it is a recurrent experience, over time it will adversely affect the development of cognitive, affective, and physiological function (Bremner, Vermetten, & Lanius, 2010) as well as self-relational capacities (van der Kolk & d'Andrea, 2010; Courtois & Ford, 2013).

Core Difficulties as a Result of Complex Trauma

Below is a description of the core difficulties that survivors experience as a result of complex trauma.

Classic PTSD Symptoms

Re-experiencing. Re-experiencing symptoms include such intrusive experiences as flashbacks and nightmares. Individuals may suddenly feel as though they are experiencing some aspect of their traumatic past and they may believe that what they are experiencing is actually happening in the present moment. A flashback can occur if the person experiences something in the present moment that triggers (or evokes) the memory.

Avoidance. Avoidance behaviours are attempts to escape any reminders of the individual's traumatic past. This can take a range of forms, such as avoiding people, activities, or any stimuli associated with the trauma.

Hyperarousal. Hyperarousal symptoms are physiological manifestations of heightened states of anxiety. Hyperarousal symptoms include insomnia, persistent restlessness, or a heightened startle response. Hyperarousal frequently accompanies avoidance and re-experiencing symptoms.

Self-Capacities

Self-capacities refers to the ability to maintain one's inner sense of identity and positive self-esteem (McCann & Pearlman, 1990). Self-capacities allow one to manage one's internal experiences, and include the abilities to do the following:

- Tolerate strong affect;
- Be alone without being lonely;
- Calm oneself; and
- Regulate self-loathing.

Altered self-capacities can leave individuals feeling as though they cannot survive alone, their feelings are intolerable, and they have no way of calming themselves or of stopping or altering negative thoughts about themselves.

Affective Functioning

Common emotions. Depression and anxiety are often comorbid with PTSD (Kessler, Sonnega, Bromet, Hughes, & Nelson, 1995). Other feelings commonly experienced by survivors include fear, confusion, sadness, grief, loss, guilt, blame, and shame (Courtois, 1988).

Affect dysregulation. Affect regulation is the ability to tolerate and modulate one's affect according to one's needs. Affect *dys*regulation is a common problem for survivors of chronic trauma, who, when confronted with a reminder of their trauma, become overwhelmed by emotions and may appear to be either emotionally overwhelmed or emotionally constricted. Constriction of emotion will occur when the intensity of the overwhelming emotion becomes unbearable and so the survivor shuts down emotionally in order to manage or avoid these affective states.

In a nonabusive environment, attachment figures teach affect regulation by responding appropriately when a child is in distress. The attuned nurturing and soothing responses of caregivers reduces the child's distress and over time the child develops tolerance for his or her different internal states.

For the child who experiences ongoing abuse, the development of affect regulation is often impaired. For the abused child, the source of safety and security may also be the source of threat and danger. This leaves the child in an untenable situation leading to a disorganized attachment such that the child vacillates between approaching and avoiding the caregiver. Without the attuned and predictable interactive affective regulation by the caregiver, the child is unlikely to learn how to manage his or her aversive internal states. With a limited ability to tolerate affect, and unavailable or unreliable support from caregivers, survivors will be overwhelmed by their emotions and their feelings will be experienced as intolerable.

Dissociation

Understanding dissociation is important for understanding the impact of complex trauma. Dissociation, however, is a broad and multi-faceted construct with a long history and multiple conceptualizations (van der Hart & Dorahy, 2009). (See Chapter 8 for further discussion of dissociation.) For this discussion, we will focus on pathological dissociation, where dissociation is used as a psychological defense or coping strategy to manage one's overwhelmed affective capacities.

Pathological dissociation is a breakdown in the capacity to integrate one's experience due to extreme stress or trauma. In the absence of stress, the mind works to integrate information about one's sensations, affect, cognitions, behaviours, and identity into coherent experiences. When an individual is overwhelmed by stress or is in an unbearable situation, dissociation enables aspects of the event to become compartmentalized or disconnected from the rest of one's experience, thus temporarily making the situation tolerable. For example, a rape victim might disconnect from her body and observe the rape as though it is happening to someone else. However, the cost of dissociating is that when one or more of these disconnected pieces of information are compartmentalized and split off from one's sense of self, it results in a fragmented or incoherent sense of self or experience (Steele & van der Hart, 2009).

The dissociative process can unfold in a variety of ways. It can involve amnesia in which parts or all of the experience are not remembered. It can involve feelings of depersonalization where the person's body suddenly feels foreign to the individual, such as the rape victim described above who observes the experience from a distance. It can involve derealization, an experience where the surroundings seem foreign or not real. Finally, it can involve an emotional numbing or complete detachment from one's feelings.

When there is chronic trauma, dissociation may become a well-rehearsed strategy and the survivor may or may not be aware that they are dissociating. Once it becomes a well-rehearsed strategy, seemingly innocuous experiences can trigger a dissociative response. Dissociative experiences range from the less extreme ego-dystonic feeling (e.g., a "not-me" feeling) or somatic experience (e.g., not feeling connected to one's body), to the more extreme experience of having a dissociative identity disorder in which the person's psyche is compartmentalized such that different parts of the psyche take over different aspects of functioning for the individual (Steele & van der Hart, 2009).

Chronic trauma or extreme trauma can cause the individual's psyche to fragment. Fragmentation of the psyche allows one or more aspects of the self to avoid experiencing the trauma so that these parts of the self can go on with the tasks of ordinary life while one or more other aspects of the self experience the trauma and thus hold the memories of trauma. This fragmentation is referred to as structural dissociation (van der Hart, Nijenhuis & Steele, 2006), and it occurs on a continuum. At the most extreme end is dissociative identity disorder, where separate and multiple parts of the personality have developed and assume various roles in the individual's functioning.

Tension-Reducing Behaviours

Survivors often employ various behavioural strategies to help them avoid the discomfort of intolerable affect. Lacking in well-developed self capacities to manage affect, survivors may use "tension-reducing behaviours" (Briere, 1992) to regulate their affect. Tension-reducing behaviours may include substance use, suicidality, hypersexuality, binge eating, overeating, spending sprees, and self-harm (e.g., cutting, head banging, skin picking), to name a few. Consequently, many survivors are understood to have secondary symptoms in response to the trauma and end up with multiple diagnoses, such as substance use disorders, eating disorders, or personality disorders. A trauma-informed approach would instead view engaging in these tension-reducing behaviours as one of the ways in which survivors cope with the effects of trauma (Chu, 1998). (The overlap between trauma and substance use is reviewed in Chapter 9.)

Distorted or Dysfunctional Beliefs about Self and the World

Core beliefs about oneself and the world are formed out of early experiences with attachment figures. When these early experiences are characterized by abuse or neglect, an individual may develop cognitive distortions out of an attempt to make sense of the abuse (Briere, 1992). McCann and Pearlman (1990) identified five areas of beliefs that are most sensitive to disruption due to trauma: safety, trust/dependency, esteem, intimacy/connection, and power/control.

Safety.   Those individuals who feel safe within themselves and their world will believe that the world is generally safe, that they are safe, and that they are able to protect themselves. Examples of disrupted beliefs include:

- I am vulnerable to being hurt and abused by others;
- To protect myself I must always be vigilant against the possibility of threat;
- The world is full of danger;
- I am a magnet for danger and harm;
- Maintaining my own safety requires extreme measures (e.g., sleeping with a weapon nearby); and
- I must avoid situations that have been connected to danger in the past (e.g., my bed).

Trust/dependence.   Those who are able to trust and allow themselves to depend on others when they need to will believe that other people are worthy of trust and others are able to meet their needs. Examples of disrupted trust/dependency beliefs include:

- I will be betrayed and abandoned by others;
- Others always disappoint me;
- If I am vulnerable to others, they will make a fool out of me or humiliate me;
- Depending on someone is being needy or demanding and will be met with rejection; and
- If given the opportunity, others will hurt me.

Esteem.   Those individuals who have good self-esteem believe that they are valued and have inherent worth and that this is also true of others. Examples of disrupted esteem beliefs include:

- I am bad, damaged, flawed, or evil;
- I am responsible for bad things happening;
- I am guilty;
- I am worthless;
- Bad things have happened because I deserved them; and
- Others are bad, evil, and malevolent.

Intimacy/connection.   Individuals who have the capacity for intimacy and connection believe that they belong and are connected to others. Examples of disrupted intimacy/connection beliefs include:

- I will always be alone and alienated from others;
- I will always be disconnected from others;

- I am different from everyone else; and
- I am not human.

Power/control.   Individuals who possess a sense of having power and control in the world believe that they have some measure of power and control over themselves and their environment and are comfortable with it. Examples of disrupted beliefs about one's capacity for power and control include:

- I must be in control of myself and others or else others will control me;
- I have no control over myself or my relationships;
- Power is about dominating others or being dominated;
- Being in control is terrifying; and
- Being out of control is terrifying.

Interpersonal Difficulties

Trauma that is interpersonal in nature impacts one's understanding of one's self, others, and the world. In an attempt to make sense of their abuse, children will often explain that what is happening to them is because of their inherent "badness." This distortion of their sense of self perpetuates into their views of themselves as adults (Briere, 1992). Survivors are plagued with feelings of self-hate, self-blame, shame, and guilt. These beliefs about themselves in relation to others often set them up for interpersonal challenges.

Survivors frequently have difficulty maintaining relationships or feeling close to others. They lack certainty about the reliability of others, which often leads to feelings of distrust, suspicion, fear, and problems with intimacy. They may feel ambivalent about relationships, longing for connection and attachment while simultaneously fearing vulnerability and intimacy.

Having a history of trauma is a risk factor for being revictimized in the future (Neumann, Houskamp, Pollock, & Briere, 1996; Classen, Palesh, & Aggarwal, 2005). In fact, it is reported that approximately two of every three individuals who are sexually victimized are revictimized later in life (Classen et al., 2005). In addition, earlier trauma is associated with more severe and complex responses to subsequent traumatic events (Bremner, Southwick, Johnson, Yehuda, & Charney, 1993), and experiencing multiple forms of trauma has an additive effect on risk for revictimization (Classen et al., 2005). Consequently, patients who present to a clinical setting after a traumatic experience should also be assessed for prior traumatic experiences.

Physical Complaints

Trauma impacts the body. The psychophysiology of trauma is a chronic state of arousal of the nervous system (van der Kolk, 1994). Research has shown a relationship between a history of trauma and a variety of physical complaints. Trauma that occurs in childhood has especially pernicious effects.

The Adverse Childhood Experiences (ACE) Study is a landmark study that has shown a strong graded relationship between adverse events in childhood and a broad range of health problems in adulthood (Felitti et al., 1998). An ACE score was calculated for over 17,000 patients in a Kaiser Permanente Hospital and medical records were examined. An ACE score was simply the number of types of adverse events experienced in childhood. There were 10 possible types of adverse experiences, so an ACE score could range anywhere from 0–10. For example, someone who was sexually abused in childhood (regardless of how often) and who lived in a household where someone abused drugs or alcohol would receive a score of two. The findings from this study showed that as the ACE score increased, so too did health risk behaviours, such as alcoholism, drug abuse, suicide attempts, and risky sexual behaviour, but also health consequences, including obesity, heart disease, cancer, lung disease, skeletal fractures, and diabetes.

Given the physical difficulties of trauma survivors, it is not surprising that there are increased rates of healthcare usage by this population. Survivors of childhood abuse make more emergency room visits (Arnow, 2004; Arnow et al., 1999), experience more hospitalizations (McCauley et al., 1997), and are more likely to utilize internal medicine and surgical services (Newman et al., 2000).

Somatization disorder is characterized by a combination of pain and gastrointestinal, sexual, and neurological symptoms that last for a number of years and with no known medical cause. There are increased rates of somatization disorder amongst survivors of abuse. In fact, one study found that over 90% of women with somatization disorder reported a history of abuse (Pribor, Yutzy, Dean, & Wetzel, 1993). Thus, these somatic complaints should be accepted as legitimate complaints of pain and discomfort that are likely a somatic expression of an individual's trauma.

The effect of trauma on the individual is insidious, layered, and far-reaching. In the next chapter we will look at how to build a collaborative relationship with trauma survivors when they present to a clinical setting.

Questions to Think About

1. How might a survivor's challenges in affect regulation affect their ability to deal with stressful situations? What are the advantages of a trauma-informed versus non-trauma-informed perspective regarding such difficulties?

2. In reflecting on your experiences with survivors, can you identify any ways in which you may have avoided asking about dissociation or missed subtle symptoms of dissociation in severely traumatized clients?

3. When trauma survivors seek help from professionals, what trauma-based beliefs might get activated? How might this affect their ability to establish a connection with a healthcare provider?

4. What standard procedures in your clinic or work setting might be triggering or might feel unsafe to traumatized clients? What steps could you take to address this?

4

BUILDING AN EMPOWERING AND COLLABORATIVE RELATIONSHIP

Understanding Relationships

This chapter focuses on the dynamics of abusive relationships, reenactments of abusive relationships, as well as the foundations of building an empowering therapeutic relationship. Understanding survivors' experiences of relationships can inform the provider about how to build a therapeutic relationship with the survivor that is empowering as opposed to retraumatizing.

A trauma-informed approach understands the themes that are common to many abusive relationships and works to create a different experience of relationships. Providers working to create trauma-informed relationships aim to restore a survivor's sense of empowerment, to work collaboratively with the survivor, and to provide the survivor with a sense of control and safety. As Judith Herman writes, "No intervention that takes power away from the survivor can possibly foster her recovery, no matter how much it appears to be in her immediate best interest" (1992, p. 133). A trauma-informed provider aims to build a relationship that is characterized by empowerment, respect, and choice.

Abusive Relationships

The Impact of Abusive Relationships

In order to establish a collaborative relationship in a trauma-informed manner, one must understand the impact of abusive relationships on the individual. Trauma affects the survivor's sense of basic safety within themselves, with others, and in the world (Briere, 1992; Janoff-Bulman, 1992). Trauma survivors have often been in relationships that have been characterized by betrayal, violated boundaries, danger, disempowerment, and a lack of control. Trauma survivors may have experienced relationships to be threatening, dangerous, violent, sadistic, exploitive, unpredictable, manipulative, neglectful, and/or confusing. They are likely to come to other relationships with the expectation of similar dynamics. Consequently, creating a relationship that is safe and empowering can have a profoundly positive impact on the survivor.

Chronic traumatization in childhood disrupts attachment, which is the foundation upon which internal working models for subsequent relationships are built (Bowlby, 1988). One of the most insidious effects of a history of abuse is that it impedes the ability to trust others. The disempowerment that results from abuse can make it difficult to enter a relationship, even a therapeutic relationship with a healthcare professional or social service provider, without fearing further exploitation or disempowerment (Haskell, 2003). The provider can be seen as a potential abuser, as someone who should be feared, avoided, or manipulated. Other effects of abusive relationships include affect dysregulation, somatic symptoms, risky or dysfunctional behaviours, alterations in the survivor's worldview and meaning system, and alterations in consciousness. (These and other outcomes are addressed in Chapter 3, "Understanding the Complex Picture of Complex Trauma.")

Dynamics of Abusive Relationships

Abusive relationships tend to follow similar patterns and can be identified by a set of common themes. Harris and Fallot (2001b) reviewed common themes of abusive relationships and identified the following:

- "Betrayal occurs at the hands of a trusted caregiver or supporter.
- Hierarchical boundaries are violated and then re-imposed at the whim of the abuser.
- Secret knowledge, secret information, and secret relationships are maintained and even encouraged.
- The voice of the victim is unheard, denied, or invalidated.
- The victim feels powerless to alter or leave the relationship.
- Reality is reconstructed to represent the values and beliefs of the abuser. Events are reinterpreted and renamed to protect the guilty" (Harris & Fallot, 2001b, p. 9).

The survivor is vulnerable to re-experiencing each of these themes in a relationship with an unknowing, even if well-intentioned, provider. For example, the survivor may feel betrayed if they learn that the fact that they have a trauma history has been divulged to other providers, even if they are within their circle of care. The survivor may be confused if the provider collaborates at times and then makes unilateral decisions about the same issue with no explanation at other times. Having secrets with a provider may feel familiar to the survivor; for example, asking the provider to not document certain information shared by the survivor. A survivor may feel controlled and disempowered in the healthcare or social service relationship because decisions are made about treatment without any input from them or any opportunity to choose a course of action. Making only a cursory acknowledgment of an individual's trauma history can feel invalidating; or worse, if the provider questions the accuracy of the survivor's recollection of abuse, it can lead to the survivor feeling as if their reality is being denied and that they are being silenced.

At a minimum, the provider should be aware of these dynamics and work to avoid re-creating them. A trauma-informed provider would go one step further and work to foster relationships that are collaborative and empowering.

Traumatic Reenactments

It is not unusual for a survivor's relational difficulties to be reenacted in the relationship with the provider. A traumatic reenactment is an unconscious reliving of the traumatic experience and has been conceptualized as an attempt by the trauma survivor to gain control or mastery over the experience (Herman, 1992). Given their beliefs about themselves and expectations about others, survivors often experience their present relationships in ways that are similar to past abusive relationships—including the abusive relational dynamics. For example, the survivor might expect to be abused and so approach the relationship with the provider in a state of fear, mistrust, or anger (Saakvitne, Gamble, Pearlman, & Lev, 2000). This can feel unwarranted and surprising to the provider, who may then react in a way that unintentionally reinforces the traumatic reenactment. Another example is the survivor who has learned to be passive and acquiesce to the perpetrator in order to limit the abuse inflicted upon them and subsequently adopts this stance with all authority figures, including their healthcare or social service providers. This leads to frustration on the part of the provider who feels that the survivor is not forthcoming about their health and health behaviours or living situation. The survivor who has learned to be highly attuned to the emotional state of others may pick up on the provider's frustration, which then feeds into the survivor's fear of being abused and elicits more acquiescence and passivity.

It is not surprising that traumatic reenactments can cause the provider to experience many strong emotions, including feelings of being overwhelmed, bewildered, deskilled, angry, or helpless. Many of the pitfalls that occur in encounters with survivors are reenactments that are further exacerbated by the provider's lack of understanding of the dynamics typically involved in working with trauma survivors. (Traumatic reenactments are explored in more detail in Chapter 11.) One way to prevent or mitigate reenactments is for the provider to create a safe and empowering relationship with the trauma survivor.

Empowering Relationships

There is an inherent power differential in the relationship of the provider with the survivor. It is important for the provider to remember that survivors are often extremely sensitive to the ways in which power and control may manifest in their relationships with their healthcare or social service providers. The provider should aim to empower the survivor whenever possible. Below we describe how to build an empowering relationship with a trauma survivor.

Collaboration with the Survivor Is Essential to Empowerment.

Elicit the survivor's perspective.   An easy way to foster collaboration is to elicit and include the survivor's perspective when establishing the goals and the direction of treatment or service delivery. Having their voices heard is often contrary to the silencing that many trauma survivors have experienced (Freeman, 2001). Instead of prescribing a treatment plan for the survivor, the provider can discuss and collaboratively establish goals with the survivor and develop a mutual service contract (Freeman, 2001). Also, when a provider provides the survivor with psychoeducation related to the survivor's struggles, the survivor becomes more informed and, thus, empowered to make decisions regarding their treatment (Freeman, 2001). The survivor can then become an active participant in their healthcare or social services as opposed to a passive recipient of treatment.

Ensure safety.   The provider can start by asking the survivor what steps can be taken in order to enhance their sense of safety. The survivor may struggle with the idea of feeling "safe," so "safer" might be a more realistic goal. Particularly when meeting with a survivor for the first time, not feeling safe is not only understandable and normal, but also healthy—the relationship is new and there should be some initial hesitation. Some survivors will know precisely what they need in order to feel safe (e.g., sitting in a certain seat, leaving the door open, or holding a comforting object). However, even if the survivor is unable to provide a specific answer to the question at this time, it is important that they know it can be revisited later on. By asking the survivor what might make them feel safer in the moment, the provider can gain some pragmatically helpful information (e.g. this individual would be more relaxed if we met in a room with a window). At the same time, the provider also communicates an important message to the survivor—your sense of safety is important to me. The collaborative relationship begins at the outset, and the survivor's voice must be seen as essential. The reality is, in fact, that the survivor is the expert on their own experience.

Establish survivor's goals.   When establishing goals for treatment, the provider and survivor should develop a mutual service contract in which the goals of treatment are the survivor's goals. It is crucial that the survivor's voice be prioritized in the creation of the contract. This entails asking the survivor for their goals—what does the survivor want to work towards? Use the survivor's language when writing these goals. In addition, by sharing some of the survivor's expert knowledge and incorporating psychoeducation into the treatment, the provider can begin to shift power to the survivor. Knowledge is inherently empowering.

Provide psychoeducation. Psychoeducation about trauma and its effects is especially important because many survivors lack an understanding of the impact of trauma. Survivors often report feeling "crazy" and can benefit greatly from having their symptoms normalized as well as learning about the long-term effects of trauma. It is also helpful to share information with survivors about how to manage symptoms, the impact of chronic trauma on development, and resources in the community that are available to survivors. (This is described in more detail in Chapter 8, "Psychoeducation and Trauma-Informed Interventions.")

An Empowering Relationship Is Shaped by the Views of the Provider.

By treating the survivor as an individual with a unique perspective and history, and recognizing the resilience and strength that it must have taken to survive the trauma, the provider lays the foundation for empowerment. In contrast, when the provider focuses on the survivor's diagnoses, problems, or deficits, to the exclusion of everything else, the survivor is pathologized and, as a result, is disempowered. Moreover, when the focus is solely on the survivor's problems, the power differential in the relationship is enhanced, setting up a dynamic wherein the survivor feels deficient and must rely on the provider, as the expert, to make things better (Freeman, 2001).

The fact that healthcare and service providers hold power in the helping relationship is irrefutable but the power differential does not preclude the possibility of a respectful and collaborative relationship. An approach that emphasizes the hierarchy within the relationship is more likely to lead to inaction by the survivor, and may lead the survivor to conclude that they alone are powerless to create any change in their own life. In contrast, focusing on the survivor's strengths and resilience empowers the survivor, promotes a sense of competence, and is more likely to lead to change (Freeman, 2001).

One model of relationships with survivors uses the acronym RICH, which stands for respect, information, connection, and hope—the qualities that are necessary to developing growth-promoting relationships (Saakvitne et al., 2000). A growth-promoting relationship is antithetical to a traumatizing relationship, and its primary goals are empowerment and collaboration.

Simple Ways to Communicate Respect and Give the Survivor Control in the Relationship

Be aware of physical space. It is possible to start giving the survivor control at the very first meeting. Control over physical space and contact are immediate ways in which choice can be provided. For example, instead of insisting on shaking hands at the initial meeting, the provider can follow the lead of the survivor in terms of what they find comfortable (e.g., shaking hands or just saying "hello").

In some situations, another way to offer a choice is to allow the survivor to choose the chair on which to sit. It may be important for a survivor's sense of safety to be able to see how to exit the room. Thus, giving survivors the option of sitting in a chair that is close to a door or one that faces the door allows them to take action that will potentially make them feel safer. If possible, initial meetings should be held in a room that provides sufficient physical distance between the provider and the survivor. Consideration might be given to meeting in a room that is more spacious. Another way to give survivors control over the physical space is to ask them if they prefer the door to be open or closed during the appointment.

Provide information.   At the outset of each appointment, the survivor should be given information about the structure of the appointment and its purpose. For example, they should be told how long the appointment will be and what type of information will be gathered or, in the case of a medical procedure, the type and nature of the procedure that will be performed. The main principle is to outline what will be done before doing it. This can be accomplished by simply laying out the framework of the appointment by saying something along the lines of "Today I am going to gather some information about your current situation, the history of some of your struggles, and some general information about your mental health, such as mood and thoughts, and general information about your life." If it is a procedure, describe the procedure in general terms at the outset and then step-by-step as the procedure is taking place.

Take time.   Time should be allotted to answer questions or address concerns. Along with outlining the information the provider seeks to gather, it should be made clear that time will be provided for the survivor to share what *they* believe to be important and to ask their own questions. In the case of a procedure, time should be taken to answer questions and address concerns before beginning the procedure. The provider should be willing to slow down a procedure or even stop it if the survivor becomes distressed or otherwise uncomfortable. Taking time to stop and talk about the survivor's present-moment experience can provide valuable information about how to proceed or whether to complete the procedure at another time.

Invite questions.   Communicate a willingness to hear and answer questions at any time. This might include interrupting an interview should there be questions about the particular line of questioning. Permission to decline answering if they are not comfortable should also be given. Questions about procedures should be answered to the extent possible.

Establishing an empowering and collaborative relationship is essential to a healing relationship. Providers should have this as a focus when beginning to work with a survivor and throughout treatment. In the next chapter we will explore how to respond to disclosures of trauma.

Questions to Think About

Antonia was sexually abused by her brother and her father. Her mother was also sexually abused when she was a child, and yet appeared not to notice Antonia's abuse or any signs of abuse. As an adult, Antonia has been victimized multiple times by strangers and acquaintances. She often feels as though she is a "walking target," feels worthless, and distrusts others. Antonia is likely to enter all relationships with an abuse framework. Most of her relationship experiences have been characterized by exploitation, disempowerment, manipulation, neglect and betrayal. These experiences will likely make it difficult to enter any relationship, including one with a healthcare professional, without fearing further exploitation, abuse, or neglect.

1. What might you do to start building an empowering and safe therapeutic relationship with Antonia?
2. What changes would you need to make in your own work in order to develop RICH relationships with those with whom you work?
3. Are there institutional pressures that you face in your work that might pose a challenge to providing trauma-informed care? Are there ways in which you can address these challenges?
4. At times, there may be a difference between what the survivor needs and wants from a helping professional and the mandate of the provider or agency. Consider how you might share the limits of your services with the client or consumer by using RICH principles.
5. Reflect on the possibilities in your setting of giving clients choice and control around some aspects of their treatment or environment.

5

ASKING ABOUT AND RESPONDING TO DISCLOSURES OF TRAUMA

It is not unusual for an individual to present to a mental health or healthcare setting with complaints or problems that they neither describe nor understand as being related to having a history of trauma. Survivors may complain of panic attacks, depression, suicidality, or self-harm, among many other concerns. Unless directly asked, trauma survivors will often not disclose their trauma history (Briere & Scott, 2006). While it is recommended that the presenting difficulties be explored first, a history of trauma should be assessed. In this chapter, we discuss why it is important to know whether an individual has a trauma history and we address some of the concerns related to disclosures of trauma that are common among providers. (For recommendations on how to conduct a trauma assessment, see Chapter 6.)

Why Is it Helpful to Know if Your Client Has a Trauma History?

When a survivor's trauma history is not recognized and taken into account, they often end up being blamed for their difficulties, pathologized, and given unhelpful or inadequate treatment. It is, therefore, helpful to know whether an individual has a history of trauma. Ideally, this will lead to a better understanding of the person and result in more effective and appropriate treatment.

Benefits of Taking Traumatization into Consideration

There are important benefits to knowing that a person has a trauma history. These include having a better understanding of the survivor's maladaptive behaviours An alternative understanding of problematic behaviour is that the behaviour is actually the survivor's attempt at managing their trauma-related distress. For example, the survivor may have discovered that substance abuse is an effective way to manage intense emotions in the short-term. Knowing this, the provider is in a better position to help the survivor consider whether there are other solutions that may be effective and less damaging for the survivor. To give another example, if an individual is cutting in order to self-soothe, the provider can help the survivor consider alternative self-soothing strategies rather than threatening the survivor with hospitalization, for instance. From this perspective, the symptoms (i.e., maladaptive behaviours) can be thought of as "solutions." This nonpathologizing way of understanding problematic behaviours can make it easier to talk to the trauma survivor about other options and lessen the likelihood of the survivor feeling judged and defensive.

When Traumatization Is Not Taken into Consideration

If traumatization is not taken into consideration, there is a greater likelihood of the survivor being inadvertently triggered by an encounter with the clinician or social service provider. Any number of negative reactions may occur. The survivor might misinterpret the provider's behaviour or motives. For example, the survivor may feel controlled, misunderstood, dismissed, ignored, or bullied by the provider. The survivor may engage in treatment-avoidance (e.g., missing sessions or coming to sessions intoxicated) or use unhealthy coping responses to help manage distress. The survivor might dissociate in the session and therefore not fully engage in or understand what is being discussed. The dissociation may or may not be apparent and the survivor's response or lack of response may be bewildering to the provider who does not recognize traumatization. Lacking a full understanding of the challenges that the survivor faces or the difficulties that have arisen in an encounter with the provider, the survivor is unlikely to receive the care that they need.

Barriers to Asking about Trauma

Providers can have a range of concerns regarding inquiring about trauma. Below are some common reasons why providers do not ask about trauma:

- "It's none of my business";
- "I don't have sufficient expertise in trauma";
- "I don't have the time";
- "I don't want to open up Pandora's Box";
- "I don't know how to ask";
- "What if they become too emotional?" and
- "I don't know how to respond to the disclosure."

Below we address many of these concerns by providing guidelines on how to ask about trauma and how to respond to disclosures.

Guidelines on Inquiring about Trauma

Whom to Ask about a History of Trauma

Traumatization affects the whole person, including their thoughts, feelings, behaviours, relationships, and physical health. Not knowing that a person has a history of trauma, the provider is missing critical information about the survivor's overall wellbeing. Given the research demonstrating the relationship between traumatization and negative health consequences, it is every healthcare provider's "business" to ask and, consequently, universal inquiry about trauma is recommended. The survivor can decide whether or not they choose to disclose. Therefore, as long as the provider respects the survivor's decision to disclose or not, there is no harm in asking (Schachter, Stalker, Teram, Lasiuk & Danilkewich, 2009). Even if the survivor refrains from disclosing, the provider has communicated awareness about trauma, a belief that it is important and relevant, and a willingness to hear about it. This opens a door that the survivor may choose to enter at a time when they feel comfortable and ready.

When providers do not ask about trauma, an inaccurate conceptualization may be formed about the survivor. Moreover, treatment recommendations or interventions may be misdirected. In order to ensure the most effective treatment, all patients or clients should be asked about a trauma history.

How to Ask about Trauma

One need not be an expert in order to ask whether or not someone has experienced trauma. Moreover, one can respond sensitively without knowing everything there is to know about traumatization. As the Violence Prevention Fund Research Committee has stated, "We know of no research to suggest that assessment and/or interventions [inquiring about trauma] in health care settings are harmful to patients" (Family Violence Prevention Fund's Research Committee, 2003, p. 5).

The fear of not knowing what to say or the fear of saying the wrong thing can lead the provider to avoid asking about a history of trauma. Trauma and abuse are topics that remain largely hidden from society and secrecy is often encouraged by friends and family members. Survivors may have been threatened into silence by the assailant (in cases of abuse, for example). Thus, asking about a history of trauma can be the critical first step in addressing the abuse or violence that has occurred in the survivor's life.

Here are some guidelines on how to ask about a history of trauma (Briere & Scott, 2006):

- Spend time developing an initial rapport with the individual. Gather information about the presenting complaint(s) and general information about their history before asking about a history of trauma;
- Ask questions in a non-judgmental manner;

- Communicate empathy both verbally and non-verbally;
- Inform clients that everyone is asked the same questions so they do not feel singled out;
- Develop comfort asking and talking about trauma;
- Use behavioural language, as opposed to general terms. Someone may not describe what has happened to them as "rape" and therefore if asking if they have ever been sexually assaulted, they may respond "no." Instead, ask "Has anyone ever forced you to engage in any sexual behaviour when you did not want to?" and
- Be aware of your own feelings about trauma and violence.

There is no single way to ask about a history of trauma. Direct questions may be a relief for one individual, but seem too invasive for another. Adapted from the *Handbook on sensitive practice for health care practitioners: Lessons from adult survivors of childhood sexual abuse* (Schachter et al., 2009) are two examples of how to initiate questions regarding a history of past trauma (p. 62):

- We now know that having a history of trauma, including child abuse, is much more common than once thought. And, there is growing research to show that a history of trauma can impact an individual's health. Have you experienced any abuse, violence, or trauma in your history? and
- Did you experience any trauma or violence in your childhood or as an adult that you think would be important for me to know about, or that you think might be related to some of the things you are struggling with now?

Providers who worry about "opening up Pandora's Box" may want to avoid the issue altogether. Asking, however, does not necessarily mean that all the details of the survivor's history will come tumbling out. In all likelihood, the survivor will be inclined to say less and not more. In the rare instance where a survivor spontaneously begins to disclose details of their trauma history, it is helpful to acknowledge their desire to tell someone about what happened and that it is important that they do so, but that this may not be the right time. Let them know that disclosing details of trauma quickly and without adequate preparation can be emotionally, even physically, destabilizing and potentially retraumatizing. This is especially true if the survivor has never spoken about it before. Offer to set up another appointment to discuss this issue more and to help the survivor plan the best course of action for dealing with their trauma history.

It is also useful to check in with the survivor during the process of inquiring about trauma. It can be as simple as asking if it is okay to continue talking about the subject or asking how they are feeling about sharing this part of their history. Survivors often know what would be helpful for them in the moment. For example, the survivor might say they have never told anyone before and want to know if the provider thinks they are crazy. Reassuring them that they are not crazy, acknowledging their courage in disclosing, and affirming that their ability to say what they need in the moment is a form of self-care are all ways to support them in that moment and in their healing.

How to Respond to Spontaneous Disclosure

Research shows that survivors often do not disclose their history due to their fear of the negative reactions they might receive, such as being blamed or not believed (Ullman, 2007). Such a response often parallels the experience of interpersonal trauma. In fact, researchers have postulated that it is not the disclosure that leads to harm, rather it is the negative reaction to the disclosure (Becker-Blease & Freyd, 2006).

When a survivor discloses that they have experienced trauma, it is important to acknowledge what was heard. Moving on to other topics without acknowledging what was shared can leave the survivor feeling silenced. This reinforces the survivor's sense of feeling alone, unseen, unheard, responsible for the abuse, and without a voice. Silence can also be interpreted as shaming or blaming.

Responding appropriately to the spontaneous disclosure of trauma is important for the survivor and for their relationship with the provider. Positive responses to disclosure include providing emotional support, listening, acknowledging the impact on the survivor, and normalizing the survivor's reactions, responses, and ways of coping with the experience. Negative symptoms can be reframed as understandable coping strategies (Haskell, 2001), which both validates the survivor and incorporates an element of psychoeducation into the discussion; for example, "Your sense that no one is trustworthy makes a lot of sense—you have kept yourself safe by being wary of others who could also hurt you." Responding in these positive ways can support the survivor's recovery (Ullman & Filipas, 2001).

While it is important to acknowledge one's reactions to learning that someone has a history of trauma, it is not necessary to go into detail about them. The provider can simply say they feel sad to hear that the survivor has been through this experience. Alternatively, the provider might convey an understanding of how the survivor feels. For example, the provider might say that they can imagine that the survivor has a lot of different feelings about this experience. Or, the provider might make a statement to convey their viewpoint regarding violence, such as stating that this should never have happened to the survivor and that no one deserves to be treated that way. Whatever the response, it should be experienced by the survivor as authentic, empathic, and caring.

What to Do When Someone Gets Emotional

Even though the survivor may not be asked to provide details of their trauma history, they might become emotional as a result of just being asked whether there is a trauma history. This is not surprising. Simply acknowledging a trauma history can bring up painful memories, thoughts, and feelings.

When strong emotions are expressed, there are helpful and not-so-helpful ways of responding. Psychiatrist David Spiegel has often said, "Don't just do something, stand there." By this, he means do not try to fix the problem in order to make the person feel better. Instead, it can be more helpful to simply listen and be a supportive presence. Emotions naturally subside; they often have a wave-like quality, where the intensity crests like a wave and then slowly dissipates, especially if acknowledged and validated. When the provider pauses and allows a moment or two for the wave of emotion to pass over the survivor while in the presence of a caring other, this is usually exactly, and all, that the survivor needs. Hold the space for the survivor by sitting and witnessing their feelings and the natural course they take. This intervention of simply being a presence can be extremely powerful and healing.

After a moment or two, it can be helpful to acknowledge and validate the emotions that have come up. For example, the provider might say, "That must have been very painful. Of course thinking about it brings up emotions." If the emotions are not subsiding, it may be important to ensure that the survivor is connected to the present moment and not lost in memories of the past. If necessary, the provider may need to help the survivor return to the present moment and to ground themselves. For example, when a survivor appears to be dissociating, the provider might do the following: "Can you hear me, Alice? It's Doctor Jones. Alice, you are safe right now and sitting in my office. I want you to listen to my voice. That's right. Can you open your eyes and look around the room? Good. Ok, so you know you are safe with me right now. Nothing bad is happening to you. Can you feel your feet on the floor? Maybe wiggle your toes? Good. Ok, just let yourself feel your feet on the floor."

Other trauma survivors may disclose a trauma history in a matter-of-fact or emotionless way. This does not mean that the trauma is not affecting them, or that it is "in the past" and irrelevant to current functioning. It may indicate that the survivor is not connecting to the emotional impact at that moment.

Dos and Don'ts

- Do acknowledge that you heard the survivor;
- Do acknowledge the prevalence of violence/trauma;
- Do normalize the survivor's experience(s);
- Do validate and acknowledge the strength and courage that it took to share with you;
- Do thank the survivor for entrusting you with this information;
- Do offer resources, including counseling resources and grounding tools;
- Do acknowledge that with this disclosure they may have more thoughts, feelings, or memories, and that this is normal and part of the healing process;
- Do ask if this was the first time the survivor disclosed their history or that someone has asked them about a history of violence/trauma;

- Do share your belief that the survivor did the best they could at the time of the traumatization;
- Do acknowledge and reinforce the ways in which the survivor has been coping;
- Do explore options for safety, if this is an immediate concern;
- Do acknowledge the limits to confidentiality;
- Do ask about children who might be at risk of abuse and be aware of child protective services protocol, if necessary;
- Do not probe for details of the trauma. You want to keep the survivor and their story of trauma contained throughout this process;
- Do not assume to know the survivor's feelings or thoughts (e.g., you would not comment, "You must really hate your father for what he did to you.");
- Do not try to get everything done when there is not enough time; it is best to book another appointment;
- Do not tell the survivor that they need to get out of an abusive relationship. You cannot assume to know the reasons as to why they have not left. For example, the survivor may be financially dependent on the abusive partner, or there may be children involved;
- Do be aware that survivors who present with a history of trauma may also be involved in present-day abusive relationships, with either original perpetrators or new relationships;
- Do not ask the survivor why they will not just leave as this can lead to the survivor feeling blamed or weak;
- Do not assume that you necessarily know what is best for the survivor;
- Do not underestimate the impact of sharing these life details with you. Even if the abuse occurred 30 years ago, it can feel as real as if it happened just yesterday;
- Do not express pity; and
- Do not tell the survivor to "stop dwelling on the past," or to "look on the bright side."

Too often survivors are disbelieved or dismissed. By asking about a trauma history, providers can communicate that they are aware that abuse occurs and has a significant impact on an individual. Responding to a disclosure of trauma in an empathic and supportive way can have a healing impact on survivors. The next chapter outlines how to conduct a trauma-informed assessment.

Questions to Think About

1. Reflect on your current protocol for conducting assessments. How might you integrate some of the trauma-informed guidelines into your current practice?
2. What barriers do you see to modifying your assessment practice? For example, are there thoughts, feelings or reactions that you have that get in the way of being able to incorporate a trauma-informed approach? Are there systematic

or programmatic barriers at your place of work that would impede the incorporation of a trauma-informed approach?

3. How might you respond to a survivor who is angry during the assessment and states "I don't want to go over my whole history again, it is too painful"?

4. Think about ways in which you can incorporate psychoeducation into your assessment.

5. Do you routinely identify the survivor's strengths and existing sources of support? If not, how might you include that in an assessment?

6
CONDUCTING A TRAUMA-INFORMED ASSESSMENT

Assessments can be extremely powerful encounters. So powerful that it is possible to make the assessment a one-session intervention with the survivor feeling better after only one meeting. When conducting an assessment, it is important to be aware that this may be the first time someone has asked the client about a history of violence or trauma. In conducting assessments, one should have a broad and comprehensive understanding of the impact of trauma so that the interview is conducted in a manner that is trauma-sensitive. By trauma-sensitive, this means being mindful of the needs of the survivor during the assessment. Below, are some general guidelines for conducting a trauma-informed assessment.

Provide Information about the Process

At the beginning of the assessment, provide a brief overview of what the assessment will entail. This description should include the following information:

- How long the meeting will last;
- What kinds of questions will be asked;
- Whether there will be the opportunity for a follow-up appointment; and
- Whether resources will be provided at the end of the assessment.

If the assessment involves taking a trauma history, give the client a sense of what will be asked. For example, inform them that they will be asked if they have any history of trauma or violence (yes or no). Then inform about the type of information that will be sought. For example, if the answer is "yes" to the initial question, then they will be asked for only the following information:

- Type of trauma;
- When it occurred;

- If perpetrator(s) is(are) known, including who; and
- If others know about this event.

Let them know that they will be warned before difficult questions are asked.

Even though the process has been explained, it can be beneficial to acknowledge that important cues of distress or upset may be unintentionally missed. It can be especially helpful to start off an initial assessment by acknowledging this possibility, particularly if this is someone who is unknown to the provider. The provider should ask the survivor to inform the provider when they are distressed so that the session can be slowed down and the survivor's distress attended to.

Be Mindful of Pacing

A trauma-sensitive assessment involves being mindful of the survivor's needs during the assessment and being careful to avoid overwhelming the survivor. It is important to be aware of the time so that sufficient time is allowed at the end of the session for the survivor to return to a more neutral or relaxed state. Speaking about one's trauma history can be emotionally dysregulating. Take time to help the survivor become grounded and emotionally regulated before the end of the session. (See Chapter 8 for a discussion of grounding strategies.)

If the survivor becomes distressed, acknowledge the distress and ask what they would find helpful in that moment. Slow the assessment down. Let the survivor know that there is nothing wrong with taking a five-minute break to get a glass of water or go to the washroom.

Metaphors to Support a Trauma-Informed Assessment

An assessment that explicitly inquires about trauma may be a new experience for a survivor and they may have preconceived ideas about what to expect and what is expected of them. A little bit of psychoeducation can go a long way toward supporting a trauma-informed assessment. Below are some metaphors that can be useful to this end.

Newspaper: Only the Headlines Please

In order to reduce the likelihood of the survivor becoming overwhelmed when disclosing details of their trauma history, the analogy of a newspaper can be helpful. Ask them to give the headlines and not the text of the article. Clarify that the request for the headlines is not due to lack of interest or not caring but to avoid having the survivor become overwhelmed by the assessment process. While discussing details of trauma can be important and contribute to healing, this needs to occur when the survivor is at the appropriate stage of their healing process and in the right context. An assessment interview is neither of those.

Swimming: Be Sure You Can Float before Diving into the Deep End

In order to establish the pacing of the assessment, tell the survivor that it is important not to jump into the deep end of the swimming pool before being sure that they can float. This speaks to the importance of both the survivor and provider knowing that the survivor has the skills and resources required to manage the emotional impact of discussing their trauma history.

Go Slow: The Slow and Steady Tortoise Wins the Race

Survivors can sometimes feel that they want to tell the story quickly in order to get it over with. There is the illusion that it will be easier that way. However, taking a slow and careful pace in gathering information during an assessment will help to prevent retraumatization. Tell the survivor that, like the tortoise, going at a slow pace will ensure that they do not get too overwhelmed to complete the assessment. In fact, going slow is the quickest path to healing.

The overall purpose of these metaphors is to prevent retraumatization. Assessments that are too intense and overwhelming can do more harm than good.

Be Aware of the Impact of Affect Dysregulation

A trauma-sensitive assessment takes into consideration the impact of affect dysregulation on the individual where the survivor may become so distressed that they go into either a hyperaroused or hypoaroused state. A survivor who is seeking support in an urgent care setting, a doctor's office, or in a community setting is likely to be emotionally vulnerable and may even be feeling out of control or on the verge of losing control. Even the *fear* of losing control can heighten affect dysregulation. Participating in an assessment, especially one that involves queries about trauma, is quite likely to stir up emotions and may result in affect dysregulation.

Affect Dysregulation Impedes Information Processing

Affect dysregulation leads to information not getting stored in a coherent fashion. When the survivor is in a *hyper*aroused state, it may be clear that they are not processing information very well because their distress is usually visibly apparent, although not necessarily so. For those who are in a freeze hyperaroused state, where their heart is pounding but they are completely still, the survivor may look like someone who is hypoaroused. When in a *hypo*aroused state, the survivor may appear as though they are registering who the provider is and what the provider is saying, but the survivor may not be fully present or cognizant of everything that is taking place. When in either a hyperaroused or hypoaroused state, the survivor needs help to become fully aware of their present-moment experience.

Using Grounding Techniques

Using grounding techniques can be an effective strategy for returning the survivor's awareness to what is actually happening in the present moment. Providing the survivor with grounding tools, such as polished stones, marbles, or other small objects, can be effective because these tools give the survivor sensory stimulation. Focusing on this stimulation can help bring the survivor's attention to the present moment and away from distressing memories, thoughts or fears. Thus, we recommend keeping grounding tools in your office. (A list of other grounding strategies can be found in Chapter 8.)

Give the survivor your business card at the end of the appointment. This is helpful because it provides a record of who they saw. This is especially important if they are struggling with staying present during the assessment and, as a result, might not be able to remember your name afterwards. It also lets them know how to contact you in the future if they have a question about the assessment process or about your recommendations.

Identify Strengths and Resources

When conducting a trauma-informed assessment, it is important to do more than just history taking and assessing current difficulties in life; it is also important to identify the survivor's strengths and resources as these are a basis for building new skills. Survivors of trauma have incredible resilience. Their strengths and resources are what will help them apply new knowledge and new skills to the management of their current distress. McCann and Pearlman developed a list of ego resources to look for in survivors:

- "Intelligence;
- The ability to introspect;
- Willpower;
- Initiative;
- The ability to strive for personal growth;
- An awareness of one's psychological needs;
- The ability to view oneself and others from more than one perspective;
- Empathy;
- The ability to foresee consequences;
- The ability to establish mature relations with others;
- An awareness of and ability to establish personal boundaries between self and others; and
- The ability to make self-protective judgments" (1990, p. 17).

There is no doubt that survivors possess at least some of these ego resources and have relied on them to survive in the face of traumatic events. Other resources are often the focus of more long-term therapy and can be developed over time.

Self-Care

Self-care is an essential resource for the survivor. Self-care includes any activity that a person does to take care of their physical, spiritual or emotional well-being. Physical self-care includes such things as getting enough sleep, exercise, and nutrition. For some, communing with nature or a higher power is an important spiritual activity of self-care. Self-care activities where the purpose is to regulate one's emotional well-being can be broken down into two types: self-soothing and relational soothing. Activities that one does on their own are referred to as self-soothing. Self-soothing activities may be as simple as taking a warm bath or practicing diaphragmatic breathing. Relational soothing involves emotional self-care that is based on connection with another. Examples of relational soothing include talking to a friend, calling a crisis line, or being held by a caring other.

Time should be taken to identify what the survivor does to practice self-care. Self-care is often challenging for survivors. It is quite probable that the survivor engages in self-care activities that are self-defeating, such as excessive use of drugs or alcohol, over-eating, or cutting. Acknowledge the self-care function of these strategies and collaborate on identifying other, healthier, strategies for self-care. Consider using a harm reduction approach to address self-defeating strategies. This entails helping the survivor come up with a list of self-care strategies that they can try *before* resorting to less healthy self-care activities.

Social Factors

A survivor's response to trauma is also mediated by social factors. Inadequate social support, socioeconomic stress, and systematic or social oppression (e.g., racism or heterosexism) have all been shown to mediate trauma responses (Briere & Spinazzola, 2005).

Social support system.   It is important to ask about the survivor's social supports. These supports are likely the basis for the survivor's relational soothing. Does the survivor have a friend to call for support? Does the survivor attend any social or activity groups? How large or small is their social support system and what is the quality of that support?

Housing, finances.   Asking about the survivor's housing and financial situation can help to determine whether these are sources of stress or support. Be sure to ask about the safety of their housing situation.

Systemic or social oppression.   Be aware of the impact of privilege versus oppression in our society and the potential impact it has on the survivor. Ask about experiences of systematic or social oppression. For someone who is a person of colour, how has being a person of colour contributed to the challenges they face currently and in the past? What impact has the history of displacement, colonialism and residential schools had for the aboriginal survivor? What kinds of challenges has being physically disabled created in a physically disabled survivor's life? These are just some of the myriad examples of systemic or social oppression.

Normalize, Validate, and Educate

Normalizing a survivor's experience can be one of the most powerful interventions that a provider can make. Trauma survivors can feel tremendous shame about their abuse and about the ways in which they have coped. Normalizing their reactions, feelings, thoughts, behaviours, and coping strategies can help them to feel less "crazy" or ashamed.

To validate a survivor, the provider must communicate that the provider has heard, accepted, and empathically understands the survivor's experience. The survivor feels validated when they know that what has been shared, including both the traumatic events and the effect it has had, makes sense to the provider. Survivors often feel alone and as if they are the only ones who are feeling the way they are feeling. Validation provides survivors with the opposite of what they have come to expect, such as being rejected, ignored, or judged because of their trauma history. It is important to validate both the difficulties and strengths that a survivor is experiencing or has experienced.

Educating a survivor about normal reactions to trauma can be both empowering and healing. Survivors can feel "crazy" because of their reactions and how they have coped. Providing education about trauma and its effects can not only lessen shame, it can also provide survivors with a compassionate and accurate way of understanding themselves. (See Chapter 8 for more information about ways to incorporate psychoeducation.)

Conducting a trauma-informed assessment can be a powerful encounter for the survivor. Along with gathering vital information, the aim of a trauma-informed assessment is to ensure a mindful, supportive, non-overwhelming, and validating experience for the survivor. In the next chapter we address how to respond to safety concerns, such as suicidality, self-harm, and ongoing violence.

Questions to Think About

1. What concerns do you have related to asking about trauma and responding to disclosures?
2. How might you respond in a trauma-informed way when a survivor starts to disclose and you only have a limited amount of time in the session?
3. After a survivor discloses a history of violence and/or trauma to you, how might you respond if they ask the question, "Do you believe me?"

7

RESPONDING TO SAFETY CONCERNS

A common concern when working with trauma survivors is safety. The survivor may feel unsafe, express suicidal thoughts, or present with signs of self-harm. Naturally, this raises concerns about the survivor's safety and places the provider in the position of needing to assess risk and to come up with a plan of action. This chapter will address assessing and responding to suicidality, self-harm, and violence.

Suicidality and the Trauma Survivor

Suicidality has been shown to be associated with having a history of trauma. Felitti and his colleagues (Felitti et al., 1998) found that adverse events in childhood are associated with suicide attempts later in life. Seedat, Stein, and Ford (2005) found that 23% of their sample of female survivors of intimate partner violence had attempted suicide, compared to 3% of women who had not been exposed to intimate partner violence. Other research has found that survivors of trauma are at a higher risk of suicidal thoughts and acts throughout their lifetime, even decades following the trauma (Spiegel & Palesh, 2008). Suicidality is often part and parcel of surviving trauma. Thus, addressing and managing suicidality is an essential component of working with survivors.

Suicidality can take the form of suicidal thoughts, suicidal behaviour, suicide attempts, and suicide. Distinguishing between these forms of suicidality is key to knowing how to intervene. For some trauma survivors, suicidal thoughts occur on a regular, even daily, basis; however, there is no intent to commit suicide. Instead, the idea of suicide can serve as a form of escape, or at least the fantasy of escape, from the intolerable effects of trauma. For others, thoughts of suicide may be the precursors to actual attempts. Knowing how to distinguish between these is essential.

Another important distinction to make is between suicidal and non-suicidal self-harm. This distinction is often determined by exploring the motivations and goals of the behaviour (Chu, 1998). Survivors are sometimes clear regarding a lack of suicidal intent, despite engaging in self-harming behaviours. For example, the survivor may clearly state that cutting helps to calm them when distressed and that they have no intention of killing themselves. In other cases, the self-harm might be intended to communicate their distress to others and serve as a cry for help. With other behaviours, it can be difficult to distinguish the motive; for example, with repeated driving while intoxicated, the potential lethality is high, regardless of whether or not there is suicidal intent (Chu, 1998). In these circumstances, the provider needs to err on the side of caution in order to protect the survivor and the community. (A more detailed discussion of non-suicidal self-harm can be found below.)

The Impact on the Provider When Working with the Potentially Suicidal Trauma Survivor

It is normal for a provider to feel anxious when survivors talk about suicide. The provider may wonder, "What is the right thing to do?" The provider may not want to overreact but certainly does not want to miss something. The risk can feel great. As healthcare and service providers, concern for the well-being of others is a guiding principle, and the fear of misreading the situation and either underreacting or overreacting is natural. There can be concerns about the repercussions if a survivor commits suicide, including fears around professional liability, as well as a sense of guilt and personal failure. There may be feelings of irritation with survivors who present repeatedly with suicidal ideation or frequent suicide attempts. This can be particularly frustrating if the provider does not understand the meaning of the suicidal ideation or suicide attempts.

The dynamics of working with someone who is suicidal can easily resemble the dynamics of abuse, including the roles of victim, perpetrator, rescuer, and passive bystander. If the provider intervenes and hospitalizes the suicidal trauma survivor, the provider may be experienced as the rescuer. For some, going to the hospital may be a relief and so the survivor may feel the provider has rescued them. However, some survivors have strong negative reactions to psychiatric hospitals and being hospitalized is the last thing they want. In those instances, the provider may be experienced as the perpetrator and the survivor feels like the victim. Finally, if the provider does not intervene, the provider might be experienced as the passive bystander who did nothing to stop the abuse (Saakvitne, Gamble, Pearlman, & Lev, 2000). In these situations, however, the provider has the option to do things differently from what was done in the past; these same dynamics do not have to be played out again. The provider can avoid getting caught in these dynamics by having a compassionate and collaborative conversation with the survivor about the situation and how to manage it.

Assessment of a Suicidal Trauma Survivor

Overcome the fear of talking about suicide. Overcoming the fear of talking to survivors about suicide is essential for effectively assessing and treating the potentially suicidal survivor. A thorough suicide assessment requires the willingness to talk about suicide. Given the fears of liability and responsibility around suicide, many providers avoid talking about it with survivors. Rationales for avoiding the conversation can include: "If I don't know about it, I am not responsible," or, "I don't want to put any ideas in her head." However, not asking about suicide does not relieve the provider of their responsibility, and asking about suicide will not cause the survivor to commit suicide. In fact, asking about suicide can give the survivor the opportunity to talk about feelings that may have been kept secret or hidden in shame.

During a suicide assessment it is important for the provider to reflect on their own reactions to the process. Shea (2002) suggests making it routine practice to ask oneself, "What am I feeling in this moment?" and "Am I avoiding anything right now?" These questions can shed light on the provider's reactions and tell you whether there is anything getting in the way of conducting a thorough assessment.

Two key questions in a suicide assessment. There are two key questions that are essential to any suicide assessment (Saakvitne et al., 2000):

1. What wish is reflected in the suicidal statement?
2. What problem is solved by suicide?

The aim is to separate the survivor's wish to die from the wish to be soothed or to have the pain diminished. What would it mean to the survivor to be dead? Is that different from the wish to no longer have this pain? With clarity about the meaning behind the suicidal statement, it is possible for the provider to be more direct and clear in their response when a survivor shares suicidal thoughts.

Specific information to assess risk of suicide. Below are a list of specific questions and types of information to gather when conducting a suicide assessment (Frierson, Melikian, & Wadman, 2002):

- Current suicidal thoughts
  - o Do they have a plan?
  - o Is the plan lethal?
  - o Do they have access to means to kill themselves?
  - o Do they have intent to kill themselves?
- History of suicidal thoughts
  - o How long have they had these thoughts?
  - o What makes these thoughts more frequent? Less frequent?

- History of suicide attempts
  - o Gather details of lethality
  - o What were the circumstances surrounding previous attempt(s)?
  - o What happened afterwards?
  - o Were they hospitalized?
  - o Did or does anyone know about the attempt(s)?
- Family history of suicide
- History of violence
- Current stressors
- Current supports
- Alcohol or drug use
- Psychotic symptoms
  - o Any command hallucinations?
- Access to lethal means
  - o Have they been stockpiling medications?
  - o Do they have access to a firearm?

Four categories of suicidal presentation and provider action.   It can be helpful to think of four possible categories for survivors reporting suicidal ideation and the action that should be considered. This is a generic rubric and a thorough assessment should be completed by the provider and the decision based on that assessment.

1. Survivors with suicidal ideation, a plan, and intent → Hospitalize.
2. Survivors with suicidal ideation and a plan, but no intent → Outpatient treatment with continued assessment. Assess survivor's access to lethal means and social support.
3. Survivors with suicidal ideation, but no plan or intent → Outpatient treatment and continued monitoring of suicidal ideation.
4. Survivors with suicidal ideation and psychotic symptoms → Hospitalize.

General Principles for Working with a Suicidal Trauma Survivor

There are several other key points to remember when working with a survivor who is feeling suicidal (Saakvitne et al., 2000, p. 85): be compassionate, be open and non-judgmental, be direct, be relational, and be clear about the limits of your responsibility and power.

Be compassionate.   Have compassion when exploring the survivor's thoughts and feelings about suicide and death. For example, you might say, "I know that you are in a lot of pain when you are feeling suicidal. Can you tell me about some of the thoughts you have when you are feeling that way?"

Be open and non-judgmental.   The provider should be open to the survivor's perspective, and non-judgmental when exploring the survivor's thoughts and feelings. For example, if the survivor talks about feeling hopeless, asking "Does it feel as if it is never going to get better?" can help the survivor to explore this feeling more deeply. Open-ended questions can also deepen the conversation, such as, "How does hopelessness affect your relationships with family, friends, and yourself?" Asking a range of questions in an open and non-judgmental way creates a safe and supportive space for the survivor to examine their feelings and the impact on their life.

Be direct.   When asking questions, the provider should balance being open and non-judgmental with being direct. Open-ended questions should be followed up with more direct and specific questions in order to gather specific information to gauge the level of risk (Frierson et al., 2002).

Providers and survivors can sometimes hide behind euphemisms without any certainty that they are talking about the same thing. For example, if a survivor speaks of wanting to "end it all," the provider should use direct language and ask if they have ever wanted to kill themselves.

The survivor might present with a direct expression, such as "I might as well kill myself because things will never get better." This type of communication, which indicates extreme distress, needs to be explored. It may be that the survivor only has this vocabulary to express distress or has learned through interactions with the healthcare system that these words tend to elicit a response.

Be relational.   The provider should help the survivor understand how their suicidality affects their relationships with both the provider and significant others. (Keep in mind relationship with pets, jobs, or other "things" that are important to the survivor). Often, it is the suicidal trauma survivor's connection with others that keeps them from committing the act. It can be helpful to encourage the survivor to envision the impact it would have on their loved ones. For instance, "What impact do you think committing suicide would have on your children? What message do you think you would be giving them?" The provider can also share how the survivor's suicide would affect them. The aim is not to induce guilt in the survivor but to ensure that the survivor considers the entirety of the impact of such an act.

Be clear about the limits of power and responsibility.   It is important for providers to be clear about the limits of their own power and responsibility. The provider is not living the survivor's life; ultimately it is the survivor who must choose whether to live or to die. At the same time, it is the provider's responsibility to offer support, protection, and hope.

Non-Suicidal Self-Harm

Survivors can employ a range of strategies to regulate affect. These tension-reducing behaviours are often self-harming in nature. Examples include, binge eating, purging, abusing substances, engaging in unusual or unsafe sexual practices, or various forms of deliberate self-harm (e.g., cutting, banging, burning, pinching, hitting, injurious masturbation, inserting objects, swallowing objects, or hair-pulling). These self-harm behaviours can be understood as attempts to regulate affect (Chu, 1998). (See Chapter 3 for a full description of tension-reducing behaviours.)

There is ample evidence to suggest a link between childhood abuse and non-suicidal self-harm behaviour later in life (van der Kolk, Perry, & Herman, 1991; van der Kolk, 1987) and that the key mechanism linking these is dissociation. Dissociation is an effective protective strategy for a child who is being abused, and this defensive strategy often persists into adulthood. While dissociation may develop as a strategy to manage intolerable internal states related to abuse, it is also an exceptionally uncomfortable experience that itself can lead to self-harm.

Functions of Self-Harm

Research suggests that self-harm serves a range of functions. A review of the research literature found support for the following seven functions of deliberate self-harm (Klonsky, 2007):

- To manage negative affect or distressing affective arousal;
- To bring the survivor out of a dissociative state;
- To replace the impulse to commit suicide;
- To reinforce the boundaries of self versus other (e.g., a mark on the skin to symbolize being different from others);
- To influence others (e.g., as a cry for help or affection);
- To punish the self; and
- To experience excitement or exhilaration.

Of these seven functions, affect regulation is by far the most common.

Self-harm is often preceded by dissociation. Survivors frequently report feeling numb (i.e., dissociated) before engaging in deliberate self-harm, which is then followed by a sense of relief or feeling alive. Self-harm is used as a strategy to bring the survivor back into connection with their body and the present moment (van der Kolk, 1996). Thus, non-suicidal self-harm is often a self-soothing strategy for those who feel they have no other way of being soothed in the moment.

While non-suicidal self-harm can have extremely reinforcing effects for the individual, it is often done in secrecy and with many attendant feelings of shame (Chu, 1998). Survivors are aware that others often react with disgust, fear, or horror, and thus the survivor tries to keep it private. In medical and mental health settings, a disparaging view of those who self-harm is not uncommon. However, it may be helpful for both the survivor and provider to know that self-harm may not be as aberrant as one might believe. For instance, it has been reported among high functioning populations (Klonsky, Turkheimer, & Oltmanns, 2003). It has even been found in other species. There may be an evolutionary basis for self-harm as a way to manage intense despair; for instance, young, isolated rhesus monkeys have been observed to engage in head-slapping, head-banging, and biting themselves in response to their distress (Kraemer, 1985). It should be remembered that self-harm is usually a last resort for coping. It most often starts in secrecy when the survivor feels they have no other way to cope (Chu, 1998). Due to the shame that typically surrounds self-harm behaviours, it is important to respond sensitively when a survivor discloses self-harm.

Assessing Self-Harm

The most important first step in an assessment of self-harm behaviours is to distinguish it from suicidality. Non-suicidal self-harm can be distinguished from suicidality by the intent of the behaviour and the function it serves. Even though there may be no suicidal intent, non-suicidal self-harm behaviours can vary in terms of how dangerous they are and, therefore, a self-harm behaviour's lethality and risk must also be assessed. By far, the most common form of deliberate self-harm is cutting, and its lethality is generally low (Walsh, 2007).

Walsh (2007) describes the following two phases for assessing self-injury.

The informal response.   Once the provider has determined that the behaviour is a form of non-suicidal self-harm, they should convey a respectful curiosity. The provider might begin with a question like "What does self-injury do for you?" (p. 1061). The provider should convey a sense of calm and dispassionate curiosity and refrain from judgment or expressions of alarm. Both judgment and expressions of alarm can cause the survivor to hold back in revealing more about their behaviour.

Assessing the details.   The provider should gather information about both the history of self-harm behaviours and about recent self-harm. Information to be gathered includes:

- Age of onset of self-harm;
- Duration of engaging in self-harm behaviours;
- Duration of each episode;
- Frequency of episodes;
- Method(s) used;
- Physical damage that was inflicted;
- Triggers to self-harm:
  - o Psychological (e.g., thoughts, feelings)
  - o Behavioural (e.g., habits, rituals)
  - o Environmental (e.g., relationships, work, setting)
  - o Biological (e.g., fatigue, insomnia, illness, intoxication);
- Social context of self-harm; and
- After-effects of self-harm, both short-term and long-term (thoughts, feelings, behaviours, and interpersonal effects).

General Guidelines for Working with a Survivor Who Self-Harms

Empathize.   The provider should empathize with the survivor by acknowledging the pain of the survivor. This allows the survivor to feel both seen and heard. Concern for the survivor should be expressed in a non-shaming way and it should communicate that self-harm is a serious issue. Showing concern might be in sharp contrast to the survivor's disregard or disgust for their own body or well-being. It indicates that the provider values the survivor and has concern for their safety.

Promote understanding of the function of self-harm.   It is important to help the survivor understand their self-harm behaviour. With more self-understanding, the survivor has the opportunity to develop and learn other ways to tend to or meet their needs (Saakvitne et al., 2000). The ultimate goals are for the survivor to feel more safe, in control, and able to make better choices (Saakvitne et al., 2000). To accomplish these goals, the provider must help the survivor to identify, acknowledge, and understand the function of the self-harm behaviours. The issue of the function of the self-harm should be fully explored.

Explore options to replace self-harm behaviour.   Once the function is identified, it is then possible to consider other, less dangerous options for meeting this need. For example, if the survivor reports that cutting helps to calm them, the provider can explore alternative strategies for calming oneself that the survivor might be willing to try. It is important to warn the survivor that, at first, these alternative strategies are not likely to be as effective as their self-harm strategies. Successfully employing these alternate options to manage intolerable states requires that the survivor has developed such self-capacities as the ability to tolerate strong affect, is able to calm themself and can regulate self-loathing. In order to reduce and eventually overcome self-harm, the provider should encourage and support the development of these self-capacities (Saakvitne et al., 2000).

In a collaborative and noncoercive way, the survivor should be encouraged to try alternate strategies, to practice these strategies even when not distressed, and to delay self-harm behaviours for as long as is tolerable. The advantage of delay is that the intensity of the aversive state that the survivor is trying to manage often lessens with the passage of time and this may reduce their urge to engage in self-harm behaviour.

Based on clinical practice and interviews with survivors, Connors (1996b) has provided a list of alternative, non-injurious behaviours:

- Symbolize the act (e.g., draw it, mark one's skin, or act it out with a toy);
- Use physical awareness/sensation (e.g., practice mindful breathing, take a bath, or hold a cube of ice);
- Distraction (e.g., read a book, go for a walk, or watch a favorite TV show);
- Delay (e.g., wait 5–10 minutes);
- Interpersonal contact (e.g., call a friend, or call a support group member);

- Imagery (e.g., imagine a safe place, imagine the self-injury, or imagine another activity);
- Physical activity/tension reduction (e.g., exercise, knit, or squeeze play dough or putty);
- Art and writing approaches (e.g., draw the feeling, journal, or create a sculpture to capture the experience);
- Expressive anger activities (e.g., punch or throw a pillow, rip up newspapers, or yell into a pillow); and
- Grounding and re-orienting (e.g., look around the room and identify colours, look at a picture of someone they love, listen to soothing music, or touch a part of their body with intention).

These are just some of many options with which the survivor can experiment. The survivor should be encouraged to practice these alternatives when not distressed and to reflect on whether these strategies are helpful and in what ways. For example, some individuals may find they feel more distressed when they journal, whereas others are calmed by this activity. Validate a survivor's self-knowledge about what works and what does not work for them. (Other self-care strategies and suggestions are reviewed in more detail in Chapter 8.)

What not to Do When a Survivor Discloses Self-Harm

Connors (1996b) identified several unhelpful responses to a survivor's disclosure of self-harm, as described below.

Do not take self-harm out of context.   It is a mistake to consider the self-harm behaviour out of context and focus on it as a disconnected symptom, such as ignoring a survivor's history and difficulties with affect regulation. Self-harm needs to be understood in the context of the survivor's personal history and internal experiences. Interventions should be geared towards understanding the particular function(s) of self-harming for the survivor.

Do not dismiss the survivor as attention-seeking.   Dismissing the behaviour as attention-seeking undermines the fact that the survivor is trying to do the best they can. With other choices or resources, one would choose other behaviour.

Do not hospitalize the survivor.   While it is important to distinguish self-injury from suicidality, this negative solution reinforces external sources of control and does little to help the survivor better understand or develop new resources. It can also be experienced as punishment.

Do not establish a no-self-injury contract as a condition for treatment.   It is more helpful to establish a plan for what to do if a survivor feels the urge to self-harm. The provider should work with the survivor to create a plan that supports the development and practice of alternative choices. Included in the plan should be what to do if the survivor self-harms.

If the Survivor Starts to Self-Harm in a Session

Below are some general guidelines for what to do if the survivor begins to engage in self-harm in the provider's presence.

- The provider should remain calm.
- The provider should share their observations with the survivor (e.g., "I notice that you are pinching your skin").
- Help bring the survivor back to the present moment (e.g., "You are here in my office. You are having a lot of feelings, but you are safe now. You are an adult sitting in my office").
- Encourage the survivor to use their senses to ground themselves in the present moment (e.g., "Can you feel the chair under your arms? Can you hear my voice? What are some of the colours you see in my office?").
- It is important for the provider to remember that the survivor is communicating something through this behaviour and is in distress. Remember that the survivor has likely engaged in this behaviour before and this is probably not an emergency. Nevertheless, it is important to attend to the survivor to ground them and assist them in finding another way to communicate what is happening internally in the present moment.

Ongoing/Current Violence

Domestic Violence

Survivors of childhood trauma are often revictimized through domestic violence (also known as intimate partner violence), sexual assault, homelessness, poverty, and drug-related violence (Saakvitne et al., 2000). Domestic violence is a serious and pervasive problem. Woman abuse is defined as "the intentional and regular use of tactics to establish and maintain power and control over the thoughts, beliefs and behaviour of a woman by creating fear and/or dependency" (MacQuarrie, 2007, p. 12). Abuse results in the woman losing dignity, control, safety, and personal power. Statistics Canada documented that 29% of women reported being physically and/or sexually assaulted by their partners (Violence Against Women Survey, Statistics Canada, 1993, as cited in MacQuarrie, 2007). An actual or pending separation can significantly increase the risk factor for domestic violence; for example, in 2001, 69 men killed their current or ex-wives in Canada (MacQuarrie, 2007).

Victims of domestic violence are over-represented in mental health and medical settings (MacQuarrie, 2007). Firsten (1990) found that 83% of female psychiatric inpatients reported experiencing domestic violence. Up to 85% of women who experience domestic violence report negative emotional effects of abuse, 45% report physical injury, and 25% report using alcohol or drugs to cope with the abuse (MacQuarrie, 2007). Consequently, survivors may present with a variety of mental, physical and emotional difficulties due to domestic violence that may not be readily identified as resulting from ongoing violence. Statistics Canada documented that 12% of all violent crimes reported in Canada were incidents of domestic violence. This number is likely an underestimate given that many incidents are not reported to the police.

Given the high rates of domestic violence, it may be prudent to take the time to ask all survivors about their experiences of violence, starting with the simple question "Do you feel safe at home?" For the survivor who is currently in an unsafe relationship, they may not feel it is safe to disclose, or they may otherwise not feel ready. Asking the question at least opens the door for when the survivor is ready to disclose.

It should be noted, however, that there is controversy about universal screening for intimate partner violence. The World Health Organization has recently advised against universal screening because there is no evidence that it reduces intimate partner violence or improves quality of life or health (WHO, 2013). The majority opinion of the WHO Guideline Development Group was that there should be a more nuanced approach to screening, such that enquiries are made for women who appear to be at risk (e.g., women with mental illness symptoms) and when there is also first-line support available. In addition, they advise that written material on intimate partner violence be available in private areas where women can safely pick up the material. The issue of universal screening for intimate partner violence remains controversial, however. The dissenting opinion in the WHO Guideline Development Group is to recommend universal screening because there is no evidence that it causes harm and most providers are not knowledgeable about the signs and symptoms.

The principles for responding to disclosures of trauma (reviewed in Chapter 5) also apply to disclosures of ongoing violence. Individuals who are currently in abusive relationships often experience significant shame. Asking the survivor why she "doesn't just leave" the relationship undermines the dynamics of an abusive relationship and very possibly shames the survivor. Instead, provide support and information to help her decide next steps, work on a safety plan, assess the level of risk to her and her children (if she has any), and link her to resources within the community. For a woman who has been disempowered by domestic violence, it is important to restore her sense of power and control in her life. Support her in whatever decision she makes, whether she decides to stay with or leave her abuser. Helping the survivor understand the impact of trauma in her life is also helpful.

A helpful resource for providers is the Responding to domestic violence in clinical settings website: http://dveducation.ca/dvcs/index.php (Mason & Schwartz, 2014). This website is a scenario-based, interactive, e-learning site that aims to train health practitioners about domestic violence and its health effects. The scenarios walk the practitioner through different scenarios, teaching them how to better support women who are experiencing or at-risk-of-experiencing abuse.

Sexual Assault

Sexual assault is any unwanted sexual act done by one person to another. Unfortunately, sexual assault is another common occurrence in women's lives. While both men and women experience sexual assault, far more women are raped than men. In fact, in 2003, 9 out of every 10 rape victims in the United States were women (U.S. Department of Justice, 2003). Survivors of sexual assault often experience trauma-related symptoms—both immediate and delayed symptoms. Symptoms can include feelings of fear, helplessness, guilt, and anger, among others. The survivor may have a strong startle response and find it difficult to calm down. It is common for the survivor to both actively avoid thinking about what happened, while also being overwhelmed by certain memories of the event. Some individuals following a sexual assault may report feeling numb and/or may struggle to remember details of the assault. Survivors of sexual assault are more likely to experience depression, PTSD, abuse alcohol and drugs, and contemplate suicide (World Health Organization, 2002).

It is estimated that at least one in every six women has experienced at least one incident of sexual assault (National Institute of Justice & Centres for Disease Control and Prevention, 1998). Many studies have indicated that individuals who have experienced childhood trauma are even more likely to experience revictimization including sexual assault as an adult (Classen, Palesh, & Aggarwal, 2005; Widom, Czaja, & Dutton, 2008). Although estimates vary, more than 50% of sexual assaults are committed by persons known to the victim (Tavara, 2006). Sexual assault may occur in forms that are not initially identified as assault, such as in situations of date rape. Young women between the ages of 16 and 24 are particularly vulnerable to being sexually assaulted—four times more likely than any other age group and estimates are up to 30% of this age group experience date/acquaintance rape (Danielson & Holmes, 2004; Wolitzky-Taylor et al., 2008). It is estimated that less than 25% of survivors report the sexual assault to the police (Welch & Mason, 2007). Reasons for this may be partly due to the cultural landscape surrounding violence against women as it is something that is at a minimum tolerated or accepted and at worst justified and glorified.

Myths about sexual assault include blaming the victim for how she dressed or acted, blaming the victim for being drunk, or dismissing the victim if there are no visible injuries. This can be reinforced by reactions of providers as well as the legal system and experienced by victims as "a second rape" (Campbell, Wasco, Ahrens, Sefl, & Barnes, 2001). Blame, anger, and shame can be internalized by the victim.

Sexual assault victims experience a loss of control and power during the assault and it is important to provide choice and offer control back to victims. This sense of loss of control can be further aggravated if "date rape drugs" were involved. The same principles in responding to disclosures of trauma (see Chapter 5) also apply to sexual assault victims. A supportive and non-judgmental attitude towards the victims is essential. Further considerations include giving her a choice about whether to undergo a forensic testing kit if that option is available; however this test requires expertise and is ideally carried out by specialized forensic nurse examiners who are trauma-informed and have specialized medical, psychological, and legal expertise. Other considerations include prophylactic medication to treat potential exposure to HIV (which must be started in a timely fashion) as well as treatment for exposure to other sexually transmitted infections and potential pregnancy.

There are women's shelters and sexual assault care centres or rape crisis centres across North America. It is important to have information about available resources.

Safety concerns are a common occurrence when working with trauma survivors. It is important to be knowledgeable about how to respond and intervene sensitively, appropriately, and effectively. The next chapter explores trauma-informed interventions, including psychoeducation and responding to dissociation.

Questions to Think About

1. Reflect on your own experiences with survivors who express suicidal thoughts. What are your own reactions to this disclosure, and how do those reactions affect your capacity to respond to the survivor?
2. What supports do you have, personally and professionally, for dealing with a potentially high-risk situation, such as working with someone who is chronically suicidal?
3. Is the distinction between the function of self-harm and suicide useful in your practice? What questions might you ask to clarify the intent and function of the behaviour?
4. How might you respond to a survivor who comes in and says, "I had a terrible night last night. I felt suicidal and thought I might self-harm"?
5. Applying a trauma-informed approach, how might you respond to a survivor who is depressed and frustrated by a setback in her job search and states, "If I don't get that job, it's no use. I might as well kill myself."

8

PSYCHOEDUCATION AND TRAUMA-INFORMED INTERVENTIONS

Given the complex difficulties that survivors of trauma often face, a stage-oriented approach to treatment is recommended. The first stage of trauma therapy is the establishment of safety and stability in the survivor's life. This initial stage helps the survivor to develop an understanding of the ways in which trauma has affected their life; to develop resources, skills, and capacities for self-care; and to engage in symptom management. Providers in many settings may find themselves working with trauma survivors at this stage. This chapter covers the psychoeducational material that can be incorporated into treatment, including information about the neurobiology of trauma, the window of tolerance, triggers, dissociation, flashbacks, and grounding, associated interventions for managing some of these challenges, and the importance of self-care.

Psychoeducation

Psychoeducation is an integral part of treatment and can be used by providers across disciplines. It can be especially powerful in short-term treatment, as transmitting knowledge in addition to teaching skills can allow the provider to have a significant impact within a short period of time. The knowledge and skills gained in a brief treatment can have a transformative effect on an individual that lasts a lifetime. Trauma survivors often feel they are "crazy," "losing control," or are "different from everyone else." Being able to explain the *what*, *how*, and *why* of their trauma-related experience is validating.

Knowledge is not only normalizing, but also empowering, and helping survivors to gain an understanding of themselves that is non-shaming and non-blaming, but rather respectful and empowering, can have a huge impact. Providers can incorporate each of the topics below into psychoeducation with a survivor.

Neurobiological Framework for Understanding Traumatic Stress Responses

A neurobiological framework for understanding what happens in the brain and the body in response to trauma is not simply educational; it can demystify and destigmatize what are otherwise confusing reactions for the survivor, and it can also inform treatment. Below, we provide some basic information to help the provider and survivor understand the traumatic stress response.

Trauma and the Triune Brain

Paul MacLean proposed that the human brain is essentially three brains in one: the reptilian brain (brainstem), old mammalian brain (limbic system), and mammalian brain (cortex) (MacLean, 1973, cited in Newman and Harris, 2009). Another way of conceptualizing the triune brain is that it is comprised of the instinctive brain, emotional brain, and thinking brain.

The brainstem keeps the body's nervous system functioning, including all that is required for survival (heart rate, breathing, blood pressure, and digestion), as well as arousal (being awake and alert). The limbic system is the source of subjective emotional experience, the formation of memories, and motivation. The neocortex is the most advanced part of the brain and is involved in spatial reasoning, language, thought, motor commands, sensory perception, and all other higher order cognitive processes. All three parts of the brain are interconnected and work together. There is also an overlapping of the roles of these three sections for some of the brain's functions.

It is helpful to understand the implications of the triune brain for what happens when a person experiences (or even remembers) a traumatic event. When under threat, the brainstem is immediately activated, takes over, and causes instinctive responses to the threat to occur without the involvement of conscious control. A person under attack, particularly if survival is threatened, does not first feel fear and then decide what to do; under attack, the person immediately acts based on instinct about the best chance for survival. Below, this process, along with its implications, is described in more detail.

Information Processing: The High Road and the Low Road

The thalamus is a part of the limbic system and the relay station for all perceptual data that is received. It manages incoming sensory information and directs this information to the sensory cortex, where it is assessed. The sensory cortex then signals the amygdala, also a part of the limbic system, for the appropriate emotional response to this information. The role of the amygdala is to sound the alarm for action, whether in a benign situation, such as when the phone rings, or in a dangerous situation, such as when the person is being attacked.

The emotion of fear simultaneously initiates two information-processing systems: the "low road" and the "high road" (LeDoux, 1996). The "high road" involves the sensory cortex, which is in charge of executive function. The "low road" allows for a quick behavioural and emotional response at the cost of any cortical assessment. When incoming perceptual information is perceived as threatening, both roads are initiated. On the "low road," the thalamus bypasses the cortex and sends the information directly to the amygdala for a quicker behavioural and emotional response. This initiates instinctive survival responses such as attachment cry, flight, fight, freeze, and collapse/feigned death responses. These response types are defined in the following section.

While the high road takes 24 milliseconds to initiate response, the low road takes only 12 milliseconds—an essential shortcut when danger is imminent! Consider the following example to clarify the difference between the high and low roads: Imagine walking in the woods when, out of the corner of your eye, you see a long, skinny, brown and green object on the forest floor. You jump away from it if this visual information is perceived as a potentially threatening poisonous snake. After you have jumped aside you see that it is just a twig and nothing to be afraid of. This entire process is instinctual. It is, after all, better to be safe than sorry. Jumping away from the "snake" only to realize it is a twig is an example of "the low road" response. Realizing, just moments later, that it was only a twig is the delayed result of the "high road" processing.

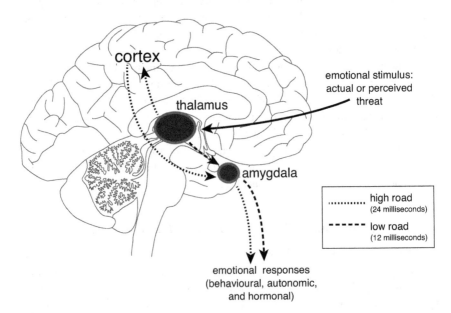

FIGURE 8.1 Trauma and the hijacked brain: The high road and the low road (LeDoux, 1996). When triggered by fearful stimuli there are two paths of information processing—the low road is an instinctive survival response and the high road involves cortical assessment.

In short, when a traumatic event is perceived, both paths are initiated, but the "low road" is quicker in eliciting a response as the cortex is bypassed and an instinctive (subcortical) survival response occurs. This type of reaction is rapid and protective in threatening situations, favouring a "better to be safe than sorry" response. The thinking brain is "hijacked" and a survival response takes over in order to ensure safety. It is important to note that this "hijacking" occurs in response to *perceived* threat; thus, it can occur in non-life threatening situations, which is precisely what happens when something "triggers" a traumatic memory.

Survival Responses: Attachment Cry, Flight, Fight, Freeze, and Collapse/Feigned Death

Survivors sometimes blame themselves for their response to a traumatic event. For example, they may blame themselves for freezing and cannot understand why they acted as they did. It can be extremely helpful in these situations to explain to them the various types of survival responses. The responses of attachment cry, flight, fight, freeze, and collapse or feigned death have evolved in order to enhance the probability of survival (van der Hart, Nijenhuis, & Steele, 2006). When a threat is perceived to be dangerous, all animals (humans being no exception) will respond to threat and utilize one of these responses. This process occurs without higher cognitive processing, which means that there is no thought, active deliberation, or cognitive assessment when these instinctive responses occur. Thus, whether one cries out, flees, fights, freezes, or collapses is not a conscious decision. Stephen Porges (2011) has coined the term *neuroception* to explain the nervous system's assessment of safety and risk in the environment. This process is important to explain to survivors who feel guilt or shame over their response. For example, freezing can leave the survivor feeling ashamed for not fighting back, or failing to act, when they fail to recognize that their response *was* an action in itself and may have prevented further injury or even saved the survivor's life. Below is a description of each of the survival strategies.

Attachment cry.   This is an active defense that involves calling out for help and may include movement towards a protector. The person is in a state of hyperarousal; the sympathetic nervous system is engaged and the person is in a state of panic. There is a narrowing of the field of consciousness as the person orients towards the danger and then cries out for help.

Flight and fight.   These are active defensive responses that mobilize the body for action (Ogden, Minton, & Pain, 2006). When in a state of flight or fight, the person is hyperaroused and the field of consciousness is narrowed to include only elements of the environment that are relevant to survival. This results in a state in which the senses are exceptionally sensitive and are geared towards locating danger (Levine, 1997). The fight response would be directed towards the source of danger, whereas the flight response would be directed away from it. Flight and fight responses occur as a result of activation of the sympathetic nervous system, and cause the following somatic responses:

- Increased respiratory rate;
- Blood is directed to large skeletal muscles;
- Tension in limbs, hands, or feet;
- Pupils dilate; and
- Increased heart rate.

Freeze. When mobilizing defenses are not possible, the body will go into an immobilized, or "frozen," state: motionless yet ready to spring into action (Ogden et al., 2006). This too is a state of hyperarousal even though it may not appear that way. For example, a child who is repeatedly sexually abused may freeze at the sound of footsteps coming up the stairs towards the bedroom. The child suddenly becomes motionless, her heart pounding as she hopes to escape notice and waits to see if the person will enter or walk past the bedroom. It is impossible for the child to successfully fight off or flee from an adult abuser, so freezing is instinctually chosen in that moment as the more effective strategy to enhance the probability of survival (Ogden et al., 2006). Freezing shares the same somatic characteristics as the fight or flight responses described above. However, in the case of freezing, there is also motionlessness.

Collapse/feigned death. When all other defenses have failed, the immobilizing response of collapse or feigned death occurs. Collapse (or feigned death) is analogous to "playing possum" (i.e., playing dead). Collapse is a hypoaroused state and is a last resort defense mechanism. The survival instinct of this response can be easily understood in the animal world. For example, the mouse, upon being caught by a cat, goes completely limp. A cat instinctively will not eat a dead mouse, and so it leaves the limp mouse alone. With little or no sympathetic nervous system arousal, feigned death is characterized by:

- Slow heart rate;
- Shallow breathing;
- Lowered blood pressure;
- Muscles becoming flaccid;
- Partial, if not full, amnesia for the event (Scaer, 2001); and
- Analgesia (van der Kolk, McFarlane, & van der Hart, 1996).

On their own, each of these responses is potentially adaptive and effective depending on the circumstances. What is problematic, however, is the inflexibility of responses or the over-activity of these responses to non-threatening cues (Ogden et al., 2006). Trauma survivors often engage in these same survival responses long after their value in enhancing survival has disappeared. These responses become patterned and generalized to non-threatening cues, which are perceived as potentially threatening. This leaves the survivor in a constant state of hyperarousal or hypoarousal, as well as causing them to feel demoralized due to the difficulty they experience in coping with everyday challenges (Ogden et al., 2006).

Information about the common responses to threatening stimuli can help survivors develop an understanding of how and why they responded as they did during the traumatic event(s). Some survivors might wonder about their reactions during a traumatic experience (e.g., "Why did I freeze?" or "It was like someone else took over my body"). With an understanding of the triune brain, the high versus low road, and instinctual responses, these reactions can be explained, validated, and normalized, and self-blame can be mitigated. With this knowledge, the survivor can work towards recognizing when they are being triggered into a survival response (attachment cry, flight, fight, freeze, or collapse) in non-threatening situations. Survival responses are incredibly reinforcing. They are what ensured the individual's survival and are, therefore, difficult to stop. In addition to validating and normalizing their experience, knowledge of the survival responses may help to open up more choices for the survivor as the survivor considers alternative ways to manage the threatening cue.

The Window of Tolerance

The "window of tolerance" (Siegel, 1999) is a useful concept when explaining hyperarousal and hypoarousal and why survivors sometimes find themselves moving from one emotional state to the other. The window of tolerance (Figure 8.2; Appendix E) is a conceptual and visual way to explain the classic symptoms of

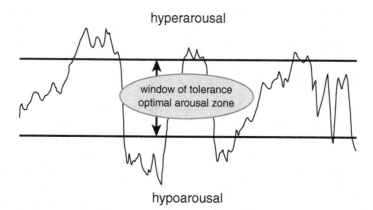

FIGURE 8.2 Window of tolerance (Ogden, Minton, & Pain, 2006). This model depicts three zones of arousal: hyperarousal, hypoarousal, and optimal arousal. This model is useful when explaining symptoms of PTSD and the common experience of trauma survivors' dysregulated arousal.

PTSD, instinctual responses, and the importance of learning skills to regulate autonomic arousal.

The window of tolerance depicts three zones of arousal: the optimal arousal zone, hyperarousal zone, and hypoarousal zone (the latter two being forms of dysregulated arousal). Triggered by cues in one's external and internal environment, survivors often experience dysregulated arousal. When experiencing either hyperarousal or hypoarousal, the individual cannot process information effectively, and it is only when they are in the optimal state of arousal (inside the window) that they can integrate information from their internal and external environment (Ogden et al., 2006).

Hyperarousal

Hyperarousal is when an individual experiences too much activation in the nervous system. The individual may report increased sensation (e.g., rapid heart rate, or sensory memories related to a traumatic event), emotional reactivity (e.g., intense feelings of fear or anger), hypervigilance, intrusive imagery, and disorganized cognitive processing (e.g., inability to think clearly, or rambling thoughts; Ogden et al., 2006). The instinctive survival responses of attachment cry, flight, fight, and freeze are characterized by high sympathetic nervous system activation, and occur above one's window of tolerance.

Hypoarousal

When someone is in a state of hypoarousal, they may not encode much information, feel as if things are not real, report having no bodily sensation (e.g., feel numb or disconnected from one's body), experience emotional numbing, and be physically collapsed or lethargic (van der Hart et al., 2006; Ogden et al., 2006). Feigned death or collapse is the survival response characterized by the parasympathetic nervous system activation, and it also occurs outside, but below, one's window of tolerance.

Expanding the Window of Tolerance

Survivors often fluctuate from hyperarousal to hypoarousal, and back again, spending little time within the window of tolerance. Inside the window of tolerance, a person can think and talk about their experience while remaining connected to their physical self, emotional reactions, and sense of self (Ogden et al., 2006). The width of the window determines how much arousal is tolerable before reaching the threshold level. Someone with a wide window of tolerance would have a great breadth of arousal that feels tolerable and during which they can maintain a capacity to think clearly (Ogden et al., 2006).

Circumstances can change the width of the window of tolerance. For example, an individual may be able to tolerate a large range and depth of emotions in the presence of a close friend or partner, whereas outside the home, they might become easily overwhelmed and hyperaroused or hypoaroused by any emotional activation. The window of tolerance can be drawn and used as a worksheet to help survivors develop a sense of the range of their states of arousal. The provider can ask them to identify any somatic indicators that tell them that they have exceeded the optimal arousal zone. The goal in working with this model is to help survivors expand the width of their window of tolerance. If the survivor takes to this concept, it can be useful to come back to it over the course of treatment. For example, if the survivor appears highly activated or unusually lethargic, the window of tolerance figure can be used to help the survivor identify where they are in the window of tolerance (i.e., above or below the window) at that moment, to explore the experience and to identify what is needed to bring them back into the window.

Triggers

Triggers Are Distressing Reminders of Trauma

Survivors can present with stories about upsetting situations in their daily lives to which they had strong reactions with little understanding about how and why they reacted as they did. When these strong reactions occur, it is quite likely that the survivor has been exposed to a trigger, which can be any kind of distressing reminder of a traumatic event. Being triggered often leads to behavioural responses that feel out of control, exaggerated, uncomfortable, or problematic in some way for the survivor. It can be helpful for survivors to understand what it means to be triggered, to identify their particular triggers, and to learn how to calm themselves when triggered.

A trigger is anything that serves as a reminder of the trauma and that elicits a response similar to what was elicited by the traumatic event. Anything that is associated in any way with what occurred during the traumatic event can later serve as a cue to remind the person of the trauma. For example, sensory information, such as the scent of a particular aftershave, the sight of a winter storm, or being yelled at, could all serve as reminders of a traumatic event. Not all the information associated with a traumatic event is necessarily stored in one's explicit memory and so one can be triggered without conscious knowledge of what the trigger might be.

Cues Become Linked through Classical Conditioning

Through classical conditioning (a form of associative learning), triggering cues become paired or associated with the traumatic event. For example, the smell of aftershave may become paired with a sexual assault, winter storms with a car accident, and yelling with an abusive childhood. These cues, even in the absence of any potentially threatening situation, can come to elicit the same reaction as did the initial traumatic event. Consequently, a survivor may be suddenly overwhelmed by a state of fear for no apparent reason.

Extensive chains of classical conditioning can form, whereby one cue becomes associated with another, which is then associated with yet another cue, resulting in distant cues in the chain being able to elicit a traumatic reaction. For example, driving on the highway in a winter storm becomes associated with driving on the highway, and then associated with driving in general. The consequence of these chained associations is that as more and more cues become associated with fear or anxiety, behaviour becomes more and more restricted.

Avoidance Is Reinforced through Operant Conditioning

The avoidance of triggers is explained by the principles of operant condition-ing, specifically, negative reinforcement. Thus, avoidance behaviour is reinforced because staying away from certain cues decreases discomfort. For example, anxiety is lowered as long as the person avoids driving. Over time, this can restrict the person's activities of daily living and make it increasingly difficult to engage in new activities.

Helping the Survivor Manage Triggers

The experience of being triggered can be described as occurring in a heartbeat. When triggered, the instinctual survival responses of attachment cry, flight, fight, freeze, and/or collapse are initiated, and the individual has no access to their problem-solving frontal cortex. It is difficult for the survivor to accurately assess the situation and a benign situation is interpreted as dangerous. Feeling in danger is experienced in the same way as actually being in danger. Once triggered, sur-vivors do their best to cope, but often end up engaging in problematic ways of coping (e.g., self-harm or other tension-reducing behaviours).

There are three components to helping the survivor manage triggers. One is to identify the stimulus that triggers the traumatic response. The second is to help the survivor understand the process that occurs when triggered. The third is to identify strategies that the survivor can use to avoid or manage triggers.

Identify the trigger. Survivors will vary in their ability to identify the specific cue that triggered a traumatic stress response. Sometimes all that is required is to ask them what they think set off the reaction. Others might know exactly what it was that led to the traumatic reaction without being prompted. With some survivors, on the other hand, it may be necessary to ask them to recall the situation and to provide as much detail as they can about what happened before the traumatic stress response. The process of identifying the trigger is important because it ensures that the survivor has a conscious awareness about their triggers, as opposed to permitting triggers to remain completely unconscious and out of their control. With this conscious awareness, they can begin the work of learning more adaptive ways to manage triggers.

Slow it down. Help the survivor examine what happened when they were triggered. Invite the survivor to recall the moments leading up to the moment in a step-by-step fashion. Ask them to describe the sensory details, their somatic experience, their emotions and their cognitions. Encourage them to slow the experience down in their imagination so that they can see how the process unfolded.

Slowing down the process and having the survivor verbally report on what they recall engages their frontal cortex. This supports a top-down processing of the event as opposed to bottom-up processing (i.e., a "hijacked" brain or the "low road"), which can cause the survivor to become overwhelmed and feel as though the trauma is happening all over again. Nevertheless, it is important to monitor the survivor to ensure that they do not become inadvertently triggered simply by describing how the process of being triggered unfolded. It is essential that the survivor maintain their sense of being in the here-and-now as they describe what happened. If they lose contact with the present moment, then it is necessary to shift gears to ground them and reorient to the here-and-now.

The Trigger Scale (Figure 8.3; Appendix F) can be useful in aiding the survivor to develop greater awareness about their triggering process. For instance, they can be asked to describe what a "3" on the scale looks like for them. Survivors often feel as if they are at the mercy of their symptoms, many of which are somatic. By helping survivors label their experiences of distress, they will hopefully recognize their traumatic stress response symptoms the next time they are triggered. Ideally, this awareness will then give them more choice in how they cope with their distress. By developing an awareness of indications that one's distress is increasing

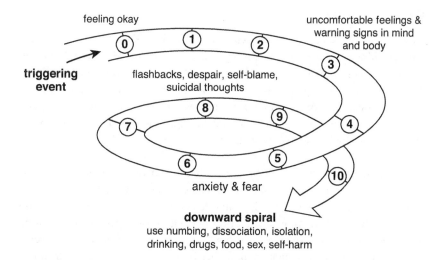

FIGURE 8.3 Trigger scale. Survivors of trauma can identify their subjective experience at each stage on the trigger (e.g., individual signs and symptoms of distress).

and learning to slow down the reaction process, the individual will eventually have more choice about what coping strategies to use to manage the distress.

Explore strategies for managing triggers. Engage the survivor in an exploration of the range of options they have for dealing with triggers. Certainly, one option is to avoid situations that are triggering. This may be appropriate in the short-term, depending on the type of trigger. For example, if the trigger is being in a crowd, then the survivor can avoid situations where there are likely to be crowds. However, as this example suggests, avoidance is not optimal as a long-term strategy. Oftentimes, avoidance is also not possible, such as when the triggering cue is commonly encountered in the survivor's everyday life, or when avoiding a particular cue will severely restrict the survivor's life. The survivor should come up with a range of alternative strategies. The survivor might identify somatic, interpersonal or other resources that would be helpful in the moment, such as focusing on their breath, reaching out to a friend for support, having a warm bath, walking away from the situation, etc. Creating a list of possible strategies ahead of time can be helpful.

Another component of managing triggers is being aware of potentially triggering situations. The survivor can either choose to avoid them or can think ahead about what they need to do to feel sufficiently resourced in order to get through the situation. The survivor might also try reminding themselves that the triggers are simply reminders of the past and that the actual traumatic events are in the past and not occurring in the present.

Dissociation

What Is Dissociation?

Dissociation is a broad construct with no single definition. Generally speaking, one can think of dissociation as a process or as a structure. However, dissociation can also be conceptualized as occurring on a continuum from nonpathological dissociation to pathological dissociation. For our purpose, we will discuss pathological dissociation expressed as either a process or structure. Whether viewed as a process or as a structure, pathological dissociation is a way to protect the psyche from emotionally intolerable experiences.

Dissociation as a process. When an individual is overwhelmed or is in an unbearable situation, dissociation is a defensive strategy that enables aspects of the event to be disconnected or not remembered, and makes the situation momentarily bearable. An example of dissociating in order to disconnect from a traumatic experience is the rape victim who has the sense of being on the ceiling looking down at what is happening to her body. Dissociation serves to protect oneself during the traumatic event by compartmentalizing the experience so that the whole psyche does not have to experience it in its entirety.

It is also a process that can become ingrained and used to protect the survivor from overwhelming feelings that are attached to the memory of a trauma from the past. Dissociation might occur as a result of being triggered. When this happens, the survivor might enter a dissociated state, experience a flashback, and later have amnesia for what happened. Another way of dissociating in the moment is to have a sense that one's surroundings are unreal, an experience that is known as derealization. The survivor might also have a sense of depersonalization during which they do not feel real. The person might feel numb, with no feelings when they know they should be feeling something, Time might feel distorted, often slowing down as though events are unfolding in slow motion. For trauma survivors, dissociation is initially an effective defensive process that serves to protect the person from overwhelming experience. However, eventually the defense itself becomes a problem as it keeps the person disconnected from their experience and thus unable to resolve their traumatic memories.

Structural dissociation.   Structural dissociation has been well elaborated by van der Hart, Nijenhuis, and Steele (2006), who built on the work of Pierre Janet, a pioneer in the field of trauma and structural dissociation. Under non-threatening circumstances, the mind integrates information about one's thoughts, feelings and experiences about the past, present and future. However, when a traumatic event happens, the mind splits in two. One part of the mind carries on with daily living and is referred to as the "apparently normal personality" (ANP). This is the part of the traumatized self that goes to work, takes care of the children, socializes with friends, and so on. The ANP enables the survivor to carry on in life in as normal a way as possible. This aspect of the personality is "apparently normal" in that the fact that they have split off part of their mind is not obvious. The other part of the mind, which holds the traumatic memories, is called the "emotional personality" (EP). Within the emotional personality, there may be more divisions capturing various defensive responses. These defensive responses are expressions of the animal defenses of attachment cry, flight, fight, freeze, and collapse/feigned death.

Someone who experiences a single traumatic event will have one ANP and may have one or more EPs, such as a flight EP, fight EP and a freeze EP, for example. This is referred to as secondary dissociation. Secondary dissociation applies to someone who is diagnosed with simple PTSD, complex PTSD or borderline personality disorder.

For someone who has been chronically and severely traumatized, splits can occur in both the ANP as well as the EP, resulting in multiple splits within the ANP, in addition to multiple EPs. This is known as tertiary dissociation or dissociative identity disorder (formerly known as multiple personality disorder). For example, there might be an ANP that goes to work, an ANP that socializes with friends, and an ANP that is married with children. Meanwhile, there will also be various EPs holding different parts of the traumatic memories. For those with histories of chronic childhood abuse, there are likely to be child EPs holding various traumatic memories and defensive strategies. There could be more than one fight EP, more than one flight EP, and so on. The complexity and presentation of structural dissociation varies widely across individuals.

As a provider, it is important to realize that someone may have structural dissociation even though the provider does not see it. Trauma survivors are often highly adept at hiding their disorder. They might begin to reveal their struggles, if they choose to reveal them at all, only if they feel safe enough to do so.

What Does Dissociation Look Like?

Even though the survivor might not reveal that they dissociate, there are presentations that may suggest that a person is dissociating. Here are some examples of how a survivor might appear if they dissociate in the provider's presence:

- Shuts their eyes;
- "Spaces out," seems "in a fog," or is dazed;
- Does not respond to questions;
- Reports not being able to see or hear clearly (e.g., reports seeing the provider's lips move, but cannot hear anything);
- Reports tunnel vision;
- Reports feeling spacey or foggy; and
- Is absorbed by a flashback or memory, or by some other internal experience.

Flashbacks. A flashback occurs when the person is re-experiencing some aspect of the traumatic event. The re-experiencing can be intense and feel as though the traumatic event is actually happening in the present moment. The individual may report having sensory experiences of the trauma, for example, tasting, smelling, or feeling some aspect of the trauma. Flashbacks are often triggered by an external cue (e.g., a sound or smell), interpersonal dynamic (e.g., being yelled at or being touched), or internal experience (e.g., an emotion, such as fear). Flashbacks are not helpful ways to process traumatic memories. Instead, they are usually retraumatizing.

What to Do if Someone Dissociates

When an individual dissociates it is essential to help them reconnect to the present moment. Below, we draw on Saakvitne, Gamble, Pearlman, and Lev's (2000) training curriculum for working with survivors.

Use a clear and strong voice. The voice should not be harsh but it also should not be too gentle. The survivor needs to feel the strength of the provider. The aim is for the survivor to be made to feel both safe and secure by the sound of the provider's voice.

Orient to the four Ws: who, where, when, and what. Someone who is dissociating may lose awareness of who they are with, where they are, how old they are, and what is actually happening. This is why it is important to address the who, where, when, and what of the actual situation, which involves taking the following steps:

- Tell them who they are and who you are (i.e., state their name and your name).
- Tell them where they are right now (i.e., tell them that they are in your office and name the city or town).
- Tell them when it is (i.e., name the present date, time, and year).
- Tell them what is happening (i.e., name the context, such as, that it is a therapy session, they are having a physical examination, or they are there to talk about their disability application).

Directed awareness. To reconnect someone to the present moment, it can be helpful to direct their awareness to their somatic and sensory experiences. Examples include:

- *Auditory*: Can you hear my voice now?
- *Visual*: Can you open your eyes and see the bowl of marbles on the table?
- *Touch*: Can you feel the fabric of the armrest under your hand?
- *Movement*: Can you push your feet into the floor to help you feel them?
- *Breath*: Can you notice your breathing? It seems to have slowed down.

Reinforce and encourage. When the survivor begins to respond to anything that the provider is saying to bring them back to the present moment, the provider should reinforce and encourage the reconnection with the present. It is as though the survivor has grabbed a lifeline and it is important that they be encouraged to hang on to it. After survivors have dissociated and are back in the present moment, it is common for them to feel confused. Help to orient them to what has happened. For example, "We were talking about the incident at work and you started to have some really intense feelings. It seemed like you then shut down. Let's focus on you being here now. What do you notice in this room you are in right now?"

Identify the trigger. When the individual feels grounded, and perhaps in a subsequent session, it is helpful to identify the stimulus that led to the dissociation. This knowledge will help the survivor develop better control over their dissociative responses. The provider can incorporate psychoeducation about dissociation into their work with the survivor. It can be relieving and normalizing to learn that dissociation is an adaptive strategy that works to manage overwhelming situations. This strategy, however, can become problematic when it becomes automatic in non-threatening situations.

Grounding

Grounding strategies are effective tools to help survivors who are either hyper-aroused or hypoaroused to bring their level of activation into the window of tolerance. It is important to note that grounding is not a form of "avoidance" nor does it "cure" the individual. It is a strategy to help modulate arousal. When someone is too activated they cannot process information efficiently. Also, when feelings are too intense, they can be overwhelming. It is helpful to modulate these strong states of arousal so that the survivor can remain within the window of tolerance.

Providers may notice that some survivors resist grounding and prefer to rush through things quickly. This may also be how they have spoken about their trauma in the past: very quickly, all at once, and with a lot of intensity. Such individuals are at risk of retraumatizing themselves when they tell their trauma stories, and in these cases, it can be especially helpful for the provider to develop a list of grounding techniques with the survivor. Find out what is helpful for them. If survivors are prone to dissociating, it is helpful to practice grounding techniques when they are not dysregulated or dissociated (Saakvitne et al., 2000).

Grounding Techniques

It is useful to explore with the survivor what they find to be effective in grounding themselves. Below is a list of grounding techniques that we have found helpful. These are simply intended as examples.

- Sit upright in a chair with hands on the knees and then push equally (hands push down on the knees, knees push up into the hands).
- Stand up and stomp feet on the ground.
- Stand facing a wall and push into it. Try to find the force coming from the feet to the hands.
- Take three breaths and slowly exhale after each breath.
- Squeeze the left arm all the way up and down with the right hand. Switch sides.
- Count the number of blue objects in the office.
- Smell a fresh essential oil, such as peppermint.
- Teach the 5–5–5 Technique (i.e., the survivor lists five things they can see in the room, five things they can touch, and five things they can hear).
- Create a grounding toolbox using items that the survivor can utilize. For example, the survivor can fill the box with smelling salts/aromatic oils, a crunchy granola bar for texture and sugar, and something that is a little noisy, such as a change purse with coins inside.

Self-Care

Self-care provides a physical and emotional foundation for healing from trauma. Healthy self-care activities enable survivors to be better prepared to meet life's challenges and provide survivors with resources to manage in life. Self-care is considered by some as simply activities of daily living (e.g. preparing a meal, having a shower, or doing house chores). However, self-care includes both physical and emotional self-care, the latter of which includes self-soothing and relational soothing. Emotional self-care capacities, including the ability to calm oneself and manage stress, are important. Providers should inquire about these areas, actively promote self-care behaviours and assist survivors in developing or cultivating these skills.

Self-Care Is a Preventive/Restorative Strategy

Developing healthy self-care strategies will allow survivors to identify their physical and emotional needs. This can help survivors to prevent crises such as sudden acute health problems that may have been avoided through preventive care. It is hard to make healthy decisions when one is exhausted or to choose new, safer behaviours when feeling depleted through lack of nourishment. Caring for oneself can also be a way of restoring balance in life. Pushing oneself by over-working while denying the need for rest and recreation may be a significant coping strategy for some survivors. Restoring a more balanced lifestyle can help these individuals to reclaim or explore aspects of self that have been denied or neglected.

It is important not to oversell self-care as a quick fix or panacea but instead to encourage practice over time; with practice, self-care will gradually improve the survivor's sense of well-being. Self-care is safer than other strategies survivors may use to manage difficult feelings, but its ability to reduce intense distress will not be as fast acting or as dramatic. Thus, survivors should be helped to notice small changes in their capacity to cope with distressing feelings when they use self-care activities. It is important for the survivor to recognize that self-care activities may not have as immediate an effect as the unhealthy self-soothing activities that they are meant to replace but that the effectiveness of these activities as both preventive and restorative will grow over time.

Why Self-Care Can Be Difficult for Survivors

Survivors of trauma often experience self-care as a paradox. Believing themselves to be worthless or defective makes self-care irrelevant for some survivors (Chu, 1998). A lack of self-care can be seen in their lack of care for their physical health (e.g., not seeing a doctor when ill, not eating well, or engaging in self-harm), lack of knowledge regarding emotional self-care (e.g., not knowing what makes them feel better when down or what is comforting when upset), and involvement in unsupportive or unhealthy relationships.

People who have experienced trauma may not have had the opportunity to learn healthy self-care strategies, or may not have had healthy role models for self-care. To the contrary, survivors of abuse may have experienced their body and mind being exploited by another for the other's needs. As a result, survivors may engage in self-harm or self-destructive behaviours as this is how they have been taught to treat themselves and their bodies. In addition to these difficulties with self-care, activities that may be soothing for some may be triggering and evoke past experiences of abuse for others. For example, taking a bath, getting a massage, or being alone in nature may be triggering for a survivor, depending on the nature of their trauma history. Practical, but no less important, aspects of self-care—such as going to the doctor—may be difficult for the survivor. For example, a pelvic exam may be particularly triggering for sexually abused women.

Survivors can also have difficulty with self-care because they are overly reliant on one type of self-care at the expense of other self-care activities. They might use a self-care activity to excess, such as engaging in excessive exercise. In other words, behaviours that the survivor considers to be self-care are sometimes actually examples of self-harm.

Physical Self-Care

Physical self-care includes essential activities such as maintaining a healthy diet, good sleep habits, and regular exercise. Physical self-care activities include responding to body signals such as the need for rest or for hydration, or recognizing the need to use the washroom—and allowing oneself to do so. Maintaining one's hygiene and living space are also basic forms of self-care. When addressing challenges in the area of physical self-care, it can be helpful to become curious about the meaning behind physical self-care difficulties and, together with the survivor, to think creatively about how to engage in this type of self-care. Consider modifying the environment to remove barriers to self-care. For example, if a survivor has difficulty taking a shower because they become hyperaroused due to the shower curtain not allowing them to see if anyone is in the room, consider changing the shower curtain to one that is transparent.

Emotional Self-Care

Emotional self-care involves both emotional self-soothing and relational soothing. Self-soothing capacities begin developing at infancy, such as when infants discover their thumbs, learn to rock themselves, or when they cry and are comforted by their caregiver. Some survivors have developed unhealthy self-soothing capacities such as self-harm, restrictive eating or purging, or misusing substances. The ability to self-soothe is essential for developing affect tolerance (McCann & Pearlman, 1990). Without developing healthier and safer ways of self-soothing, it is difficult to manage stress and emotional upsets without feeling either too much or nothing at all.

Emotional self-soothing. Emotional self-soothing can include meditation and breathing exercises, positive self-talk, and affirmations, as well as engaging in pleasurable or calming activities, such as mindfully drinking herbal tea, taking a warm bath, art-making, doing jigsaw puzzles, walking in nature, or listening to music. The provider should help the survivor generate a list of activities that they can engage in that are emotionally soothing. It can be helpful to have such a list for those moments when the survivor lacks the emotional resources to think creatively about how to look after themselves in the moment.

Relational soothing. Relational soothing involves being soothed through connection with another, such as talking with a friend, being hugged, or spending time with loved ones. Relational soothing is a basic human need as we are wired for social connection. This is based in the dependency of the infant on others for survival. When the adults on whom the survivor depends are unable or unwilling to provide sufficient relational soothing, the infant—and later, the child—may develop their own methods of meeting this need. For example, a survivor may have an intense longing for connection and feel unable to be alone. This survivor may chronically feel as though no one can ever meet this need and that they will always be let down. This may lead to the survivor seeming "clingy" or overly dependent. On the other hand, some survivors may have an intense distrust of others and, as a result, avoid seeking comfort from others or have difficulty letting others know when they are struggling and in need of support.

Providers can help survivors identify safe people in their lives to whom they can turn for support. Helping survivors explore what makes a person safe and what is evidence that a person is not safe is important. Sometimes survivors can be confused about how to judge whether someone is safe, especially when their experiences have involved being taken advantage of by a supposedly trusted figure. As a result, they may have learned not to trust their own opinions or instincts. It may be important to challenge any "all or nothing" beliefs about safety, such as the belief that no one can be trusted or that only one particular person is safe. It may be helpful to identify different roles that these safe people can play, such as being someone to provide emotional support, instrumental support (e.g., someone with whom you can go grocery shopping), or just being someone with whom they can do safe activities.

Self-Care Worksheets

It can be helpful to engage the survivor in an exploration of the resources which they already have, both internally and externally, and which they can access. Doing this work when the survivor is not in a state of distress will help set the stage for engaging in healthy self-care activities as both a preventive strategy as well as a restorative strategy. Self-care worksheets on self-soothing strategies and relaxation strategies can be found in the appendices D and F, respectively.

Engaging in self-care supports living in the optimal arousal zone of the window of tolerance. It is through the practice of self-care, including not just physical self-care but also self-soothing and relational soothing, that survivors can learn through experience how to expand their window of tolerance and how to become more present in their lives.

This chapter has included psychoeducation material that can be used to support the survivor to better understand the impact of trauma on themselves. In addition, by responding appropriately and effectively to dissociation, the provider can help the survivor develop skills to manage their affect dysregulation. And lastly, by helping the survivor learn the essential skills of self-care, the survivor can use these tools as both a restorative and preventive strategy in their daily life.

Questions to Think About

1. Sarah comes in complaining of depression. She has recently started a new job, and she has a boss who is a bully. When he sexually harassed Sarah, she froze and then quit her job the next day. As a child, she lived with parents who were violent alcoholics. When her parents drank they would become unpredictably enraged and beat her. To protect herself, Sarah would hide in closets and try to be as still as possible. How might you normalize her reactions to trauma? What psychoeducational tools might be helpful to Sarah?

2. Dale has a history of having difficulty keeping a job and has anger management problems, particularly with authority figures. Dale grew up poor and was physically abused and neglected as a child. In addition to this, he was bullied at school. As an adult, he often isolates himself. How would a trauma-informed lens help you to understand his behaviour? What psychoeducational tools might be helpful to Dale?

3. How might you respond to a survivor who reports that grounding is unhelpful because it does not compare to how good using substances makes her feel?

9
DEALING WITH SUBSTANCE USE

A chapter dedicated to substance use disorders has been included in this book to highlight the prevalence of substance use with trauma survivors. Twenty-four percent of patients with anxiety disorders (including PTSD) struggle with substance use disorders (Regier et al., 1984). Substance use disorders may alter the treatment outcomes of PTSD and other anxiety disorders (Compton, 2007; Kessler, Chiu, Demler, & Walters, 2005).

It is not uncommon for a trauma survivor presenting to mental health and healthcare settings, as well as social services, to use one or more recreational substances, prescription medications, or over-the-counter medications to cope with their situation and to self-medicate their symptoms. Unfortunately, what initially starts as a mechanism for escaping fears and psychic pain, or for avoiding the re-experiencing of symptoms, may worsen the survivor's ability to modulate affect. What may have begun as a coping mechanism can develop into separate medical, social, and psychiatric problems. It may lead to legal problems, negatively affect fulfillment of role obligations, be physically hazardous, or interfere with social and interpersonal relationships (American Psychiatric Association, 2013).

The survivor may not recognize that their pattern of substance use constitutes abuse or dependence or that the use has a worsening effect on their symptoms. For both the survivor and provider, it may be difficult to decide which symptoms are due to the direct effect of, or withdrawal from, the substance in question, and which ones are a product of a primary psychiatric disorder (such as depression or anxiety). This is often the reason why trauma survivors are seen as so complex and why diagnostic models may fail them. In all cases, it is critical to give attention to the substance use disorder as it will be very difficult to address other problems if substance use dominates the clinical picture.

The focus of this chapter is on how to assist survivors who are using substances, how to help identify what could be contributing to their current distress, how to assess their level of distress, and how to intervene effectively. It may be a question of stabilizing and managing substance intoxication or managing withdrawal symptoms and giving medical care rather than starting a long-term therapy program. For this reason, we have focused this chapter on assessment, recognizing symptoms of substance abuse and dependence, understanding the basic concepts of motivational interviewing and stages of change, as well as withdrawal management strategies for alcohol and benzodiazepines (as these are commonly encountered in a clinical setting and can lead to serious complications). Management strategies for other substances will be discussed briefly.

Assessment

General Guidelines

The survivor may not be aware of the amount of alcohol or drugs they are consuming, they may feel shame and guilt, or they may feel that substance use is their only coping mechanism. Especially with trauma survivors, gentle exploration early on in the treatment may be useful in establishing rapport. Substance use can be explored later, in more detail, over the course of two to three sessions.

It is important to assess and address substance use early on in treatment. If it is not addressed, it will likely interfere with or halt any progress that is made. In certain clinical settings, stabilization may mean addressing substance use first and then preparing the individual to participate in longer-term treatment to address the effects of chronic trauma.

In the first assessment, obtain a thorough substance use history. Normalize the interview at the beginning of the assessment by stating that these are routine questions that are asked of everyone. Remember that not asking about substance use only leads to a delay in effective treatment. Ask about substance use often throughout treatment. Ask direct and specific questions.

Consider the following when discussing substance use in general: adopt a nonjudgmental attitude; assume a tactfully persistent approach; avoid labels such as "alcoholic" or "drug user," unless the individual uses them and leading questions may be useful. Occasional use of leading questions can help achieve a more accurate history and normalize behaviours so that the individual feels comfortable answering. An example of a leading question might be, "How many drinks do you have in a week, 20 or more like 40?" as opposed to asking the question, "Do you drink alcohol?" This may be helpful in situations where the individual is struggling to be authentic because of shame or guilt. Include questions about substance abuse as normal everyday behaviour along with questions about diet and exercise. It is often easier to transition from asking about caffeine use to alcohol use in a given week than to open the discussion with "How much do you drink in a week?"

Record substance intake in standard measurements. Individuals may under-estimate their own alcohol intake if they use large glasses. Ask the survivor to demonstrate how much of the glass the alcohol takes up. Keep in mind that alcohol content will differ based on the type of drink consumed. For example a standard drink of beer or a cooler (340mL or 12oz) contains approximately 5% alcohol but a standard glass of wine is 140mL (5oz) and contains approximately 12% alcohol. A standard amount of spirits is 43mL (1.5oz) and contains approximately 40% alcohol (Kahan & Wilson, 2001). Depending on the type of drink and whether the individual is mixing their own drinks, a mixed drink may have anywhere between one and three standard drinks in a serving.

Before addressing substance use with the survivor, it is important to have a thorough understanding of what they are using, the extent of their use and its impact on functioning. Thus, a good assessment is essential. Part of completing a good assessment is determining if the survivor meets criteria for a substance use disorder as defined by the DSM-5. Keep in mind that substance use should be re-explored throughout treatment, as the survivor may not feel comfortable admitting to it in the first few sessions.

According to the DSM-5, a substance use disorder should be considered if the pattern of substance use is problematic and leads to significant impairment or distress and the individual develops tolerance or withdrawal from using the substance. Inordinate time spent trying to acquire the substance, using the substance despite persistent negative consequences (e.g., legal charges, loss of relationships or employment), strong cravings, and continued use despite health consequences are all signs of a substance use disorder (American Psychiatric Association, 2013).

What Types of Substances Are Used?

Routinely ask about caffeine, nicotine (cigarettes or chewing tobacco), alcohol, cocaine (powder or crack), stimulants (amphetamines or crystal methamphetamine), hallucinogens (ecstasy, mushrooms, LSD, or PCP), cannabis (marijuana, hash, or hash oil), opiates (heroin, oxycodone, morphine, codeine, or methadone), sedative/hypnotics (benzodiazepines), and inhalants (glue or solvents).

Do not forget to ask about over-the-counter medications, such as dimenhydrinate (Gravol) or diphenhydramine (Benadryl) taken in excess, or prescribed medications, such as benzodiazepines, taken in larger quantities than prescribed.

Quantities, Duration of Use, and Mode of Administration

It is important to quantify the amount that the individual is using in a given week or day for each individual substance. Always ask when they last used the substance.

Duration of an individual's substance use is also important to explore since it will provide insight into the barriers that the survivor faces when they try to stop using. The mode of administration of the drug (oral, inhaled, or intravenous) provides information about severity. Intravenous administration of the drug is usually related to higher rates of infection transmission, greater severity of use, and increased risk of medical co-morbidities.

Pattern and Context of Substance Use and Other Drugs Used

Important questions to ask include: When was the first time the survivor tried the substance? When did they last use the substance? When did the use escalate and become an issue? When did they start noticing tolerance to the drug? Do they ever drink during the day? What other drugs are they also using (since poly-substance use is common)? Does their partner use substances, and do they use substances together?

Signs and Symptoms of Past Withdrawal

Both alcohol and benzodiazepine withdrawal can be life threatening. Conduct a thorough assessment of previous withdrawal symptoms with all substances that the survivor may be using, especially alcohol and benzodiazepines. With alcohol use, it is important to know if the survivor has ever had delirium tremens (violent shaking in withdrawal which is usually brought to medical attention), seizures when they have withdrawn from alcohol, or blackouts (losing memory for pieces of time while intoxicated). If they had any of the above symptoms be extremely cautious that they will not abruptly stop their use. Abrupt discontinuation of alcohol or benzodiazepines for someone who is a daily drinker can lead to severe withdrawal symptoms or seizures. Benzodiazepine and alcohol withdrawal will likely require admittance to a medical detox facility or close supervision by their physician. All other substance withdrawals can be managed in a non–medical detox or outpatient setting, except if the survivor is elderly or medically unwell.

Physical Health Consequences

The provider should be aware of any physical health consequences related to the survivor's substance use. Ask about infections such a hepatitis B or C, or HIV. They may have been exposed to infections secondary to the risky behaviours they engaged in while intoxicated (e.g., sexually transmitted infections such as syphilis, chlamydia, or gonorrhea).

Risk-Taking Behaviour and Duty to Report

Explore any risk-taking behaviours that may be associated with substance use. Ask about driving while impaired, excessive spending, increased number of sexual partners, or any unprotected sexual activity. Physicians have a "duty to report" in most jurisdictions if their patient is driving while impaired. Physicians must report cases of motor vehicle operators, pilots, air traffic controllers and railway operators if they are working while impaired. Ask about the safety of children or vulnerable people in their care.

Ongoing substance abuse or dependence is a risk factor for suicide completion and should be explored in detail when asking about safety. Identify high-risk safety situations by asking the following questions: Where? When? With whom? Doing what? Feeling what? Consider the survivor's safety and the possible need for certification or hospitalization if they become so severely impaired while intoxicated or in withdrawal that they become a danger to themselves or to others. There has to be an imminent risk of harm to themselves or others before hospitalization is considered.

The provider should also explore the survivor's attempts to reduce or stop use. What resources (e.g., AA, NA, residential treatments, etc.) has the survivor accessed in the past? What was their experience in treatment? What worked for them in treatment? Were there any downsides to treatment? This will help to understand what tools the survivor already has. If they were able to have periods of reduced substance use or abstinence from substances, what coping strategies did they utilize during that time? How long were they able to maintain reduced substance use or abstinence? What triggered their relapse? In addition, explore what they like about their substance use. What are the downsides to using substances? What problems have they had when they have used drugs?

Identify the Stage of Change: Pre-contemplation, Contemplation, Preparation, Action, or Maintenance

It is important to assess the individual's readiness for change and willingness to access help. This can be done using Prochaska's Stages of Change Model (Prochaska, DiClemente, & Norcross, 1992). Within this model, precontemplation, contemplation, preparation, action, and maintenance are the five stages of change. This will be described later in the chapter in more detail.

Motivational interviewing (MI) techniques are employed to explore the possibility of change and to help an individual move from contemplation to action with respect to their substance use. MI is a client-centred, "collaborative conversation style for strengthening a person's own motivation to change" (Miller & Rollnick, 2012, p. 24) by examining and resolving ambivalence. Motivational interviewing uses collaborative techniques to help engage the individual's own motivation to change rather than applying external or coercive methods. Motivational interviewing and motivational enhancement are good clinical skills to develop, and can be particularly useful when addressing the survivor's resistance towards treatment.

Physical Manifestations of Substance Use or Withdrawal

It is important when completing the assessment to pay attention not only to what the survivor is saying, but also to their appearance and behaviour to get a better sense of the impact of their substance use. If they currently appear intoxicated, it is important to be up front with them and ask them if they used prior to your appointment. It is not useful to proceed with a regular assessment and not attend to the signs of substance use. During substance intoxication or withdrawal, judgment will likely be impaired; they may not be able to give a reliable history regarding other areas of their life. Therefore, it is important to acknowledge and explore their substance use. Outlined below are some physical signs and symptoms indicating intoxication, withdrawal, and prolonged use for various substances.

Alcohol and sedative (benzodiazepine) intoxication. Impaired judgment, slurred speech, unsteady gait, poor coordination, nystagmus (involuntary eye movements), and impairment in attention and memory may be exhibited. This can progress to stupor or coma.

Alcohol and benzodiazepine withdrawal. Alcohol and benzodiazepine withdrawal can be life-threatening if the alcohol or benzodiazepine use has been heavy or prolonged. Both classes of substances produce the same serious withdrawal syndrome. In withdrawal, autonomic hyperactivity (paroxysmal sweats, tachycardia, mydriasis [dilation of the pupils], and hypertension), tremulousness, insomnia, nausea, and vomiting may occur. Visual, auditory, or tactile hallucinations may be present, and anxiety, headache, disorientation, and agitation may also occur. Seizures are a risk if the survivor has had a history of prolonged alcohol use or a past history of withdrawal seizures. If extraocular movements are present, rule out Wernicke's encephalopathy (a severe neurological disorder secondary to a nutritional deficiency caused by years of alcohol use). Suicidal ideation may also be present and should always be explored.

Tremor is usually the first symptom of withdrawal and often the most reliable indicator of continued withdrawal. It usually occurs 6–8 hours after alcohol cessation, and is the last symptom to resolve. Autonomic hyperactivity occurs within 8–12 hours of alcohol cessation. Risk of seizures is highest in the first 12–72 hours but may occur up to seven days after withdrawal begins. Hallucinations and disorientation can occur within the first seven days. Withdrawal delirium can start as early as day three and seriously medically ill patients may be more at risk. They should also be monitored for arrhythmias.

Cannabis intoxication. Recent use of cannabis may be indicated by slowed speech and movements, or uncoordinated movements. There may be conjunctival injection (reddened eyes), an increased appetite, dry mouth, tachycardia, impaired judgment, anxiety, social withdrawal, or paranoia symptoms.

There is no severe withdrawal state for cannabis, but some people experience mild withdrawal with heavy use, which typically resolves within a few days. It is often used with alcohol, cocaine, and nicotine and may be laced with PCP, hallucinogens, or opioids. People who regularly use cannabis may report mild forms of depression, anxiety, lethargy, or paranoia. Cannabis smoke is irritating to the airway and contains even larger amounts of carcinogens than tobacco and can cause sinusitis, pharyngitis, and bronchitis with a persistent cough, and it can progress to pulmonary dysplasia. With chronic, heavy use, there is a reduction in the pleasurable effects of the drug.

Cocaine/amphetamine intoxication.   If a person is intoxicated on cocaine or amphetamines, they may present as agitated or euphoric, their pupils will likely be dilated, and their blood pressure and heart rate will be higher than normal (it can occasionally fall lower than normal). They may also present with sweating (diaphoresis), chills, tremors, nausea, vomiting and confusion, or occasionally psychosis (this is more common with amphetamines). Individuals may present as hypervigilant, have a labile affect, and may be irritable, angry, tense, hypersensitive, or even paranoid. They may be hyper-talkative, grandiose, and have stereotyped and repetitive behaviour. If they are complaining of chest pain and have recently taken cocaine, they need to be assessed urgently in the ER. In rare cases, individuals may present with dystonic reactions, dyskinesias (abnormal movements), or seizures.

People addicted to cocaine may spend large amounts of money on the drug within a very short period of time (the half-life of cocaine is less than 60 minutes). It is usually inhaled, injected, or smoked. If the person is routinely smoking cocaine or crack, they may have sinusitis, irritation, or nose bleeds, and is also at risk for respiratory problems due to irritation of the respiratory tract (DSM-IV-TR; American Psychiatric Association, 2000).

Cocaine/amphetamine withdrawal.   The early phase of cocaine withdrawal lasts up to 48 hours and is characterized by increased sleep, increased appetite and food consumption, fatigue, agitation, dysphoric mood, and unpleasant or vivid dreams. The later stage of cocaine withdrawal can last weeks and sometimes more than months. It is characterized by depressed mood, insomnia, irritability, and increased drug cravings. Anhedonia (the inability to experience pleasure, despite participating in activities or experiences that usually elicit pleasure) diminishes over months, but individuals may experience periodic cravings for years, thus leaving them susceptible to relapse. Individuals are at higher risk for suicide completion during the withdrawal phase.

Hallucinogen intoxication and persistent symptoms.   Hallucinogen intoxication may involve geometric hallucinations, false perceptions of movement in their peripheral visual fields, flashes of colour, intensified colours, trails of images of moving objects, halos around objects, macropsia (objects appear larger than normal) and micropsia (objects appear smaller than normal). Tachycardia, depersonalization, derealization, blurred vision and synesthesias (experiencing one sensation linked with another; for example, the number 6 is experienced as always red) may occur.

Individuals may re-experience these symptoms long after they have used the drug; however, there is no clear withdrawal syndrome identified. Ecstasy (MDMA) and LSD are the most commonly used of the hallucinogens. Ecstasy is used commonly as a "club drug" and at raves. The intoxication may be prolonged if the person uses frequent doses during an episode.

Inhalant intoxication. Inhalant intoxication may involve dizziness, in-coordination, slurred speech, apathy, unsteady gait, lethargy, confusion, belligerence, assaultiveness, or euphoria. Nystagmus (involuntary eye movement), depressed reflexes, psychomotor retardation, diplopia (blurred vision), or tremor may also be present. In some cases, individuals experience perceptual abnormalities and the intoxication state may progress to stupor or coma.

Most commonly, inhalants are used by adolescents in group settings; however, isolated use likely indicates severity of use and prolonged exposure. Men account for 70–80% of inhalant-related emergency room visits (American Psychiatric Association, 2000).

Nicotine withdrawal. Nicotine withdrawal usually occurs within 24 hours of stopping smoking or nicotine use. Withdrawal symptoms include dysphoric mood, insomnia, anxiety, poor concentration, irritability, agitation, or poor frustration tolerance. Over the long term, lowered heart rates, increased appetite, and weight gain have been reported. Withdrawal symptoms typically peak in the first four days, with most residual symptoms tapering off within four weeks. However, hunger and weight gain may persist for longer than six months.

Opioid intoxication. Opioid intoxication presents with constricted pupils, shallow and slowed breathing, extreme sleepiness, or loss of alertness that may progress to a decreased level of consciousness and breathing cessation. Acute and chronic opioid use is associated with reduced bodily secretions, which cause chronically dry mouth and nose, and slowing of GI motility (constipation). If they are using IV opioids, they may have track marks and sclerosed veins that are visible. Individuals may have cellulitis or abscesses and are much more vulnerable to infections such as tuberculosis, endocarditis, hepatitis, and HIV infection.

Opioid withdrawal. Withdrawal symptoms following the use of opioids can present within 6–12 hours and usually peak within 2–3 days, but may last up to 10 days. The insomnia, dysphoric mood, and cravings may last months. Individuals may present with lacrimation (secretion of tears), rhinorrea (runny nose), piloerection, diarrhea, nausea, chills, autonomic instability, and myalgias (muscle aches). Individuals should be warned of losing tolerance to the opioid, as they are susceptible to overdose if they use their usual dose after having withdrawn from the opioid. Pregnant women are susceptible to miscarriage or premature labor if they go into opioid withdrawal.

PCP (phencyclidine) intoxication. Intoxication usually occurs within one hour of using PCP, but the effect can last up to 24 hours. PCP use is more common in men, usually between the ages of 20 and 40 years. Men comprise approximately 75% of patients who present to the ER with PCP intoxication (American Psychiatric Association, 2000).

At lower doses, symptoms include vertigo, ataxia, vertical or horizontal nystagmus, mild elevations in blood pressure or heart rate, euphoria, affective flattening, delayed reaction time, and lack of concern. At moderate doses, individuals may experience disorganized thinking, impulsivity, agitation, belligerence, depersonalization, hyperacusis (sensitized hearing), muscle rigidity, and dysarthria. Individuals may become violent. At high doses, individuals are at risk of amnesia, seizures, respiratory depression, and coma.

Lab Investigations and Vital Signs

Medical investigations are included in the assessment section of this chapter, as they are invaluable in assessing the physical health effects of the substance use and help guide treatment. In addition, due to shame, guilt or lack of awareness, some individuals may minimize or deny their substance use and its effects on their lives. Investigations can provide objective evidence of use and help clinicians accurately assess the impact of substance use on their overall health and functioning. Individuals may assume that treating the underlying trauma symptoms will automatically solve their substance use problem. Unfortunately, this is not usually the case and both have to be attended to before either is likely to improve.

Vital signs (blood pressure, heart rate, respiratory rate, temperature). Tachycardia and hypertension commonly accompany withdrawal states and some intoxication states. Dehydration may be a concern, especially in severe withdrawal states such as those seen with alcohol or benzodiazepine withdrawal. Having three or more drinks per day increases the risk of hypertension (high blood pressure) from baseline.

Blood alcohol level (BAC) mmol/L. BAC depends on body weight, gender, and metabolic rate. Blood alcohol declines at a rate of 3.2–5.4 mmol/L (or approximately one drink) per hour. The connection between the BAC level and clinical signs is affected by the user's tolerance to alcohol. Someone with a high tolerance may not be intoxicated despite having a much higher blood alcohol level, compared with someone without any tolerance to alcohol. Non-tolerant drinkers will likely show signs of intoxication after having two to three drinks in an hour, but the drinker with a high tolerance to alcohol may actually look sober or even appear to be in withdrawal.

Complete blood count (CBC). Those who engage in chronic alcohol use, anemia (low hemoglobin) with an enlarged mean cell volume (MCV) may be present.

MCV can also be elevated by medications, folate, B12 deficiency, liver disease, or hypothyroidism. Chronic drug use may be associated with malnutrition and an anemia of chronic disease. Thrombocytopenia (low platelets) secondary to alcohol-induced bone-marrow suppression is usually mild and resolves within a few weeks of abstinence. However, if the thrombocytopenia is secondary to splenomegaly, it will not remit with abstinence and needs to be followed by a physician.

Electrolytes (sodium, potassium, chloride, and bicarbonate). Hypokalemia is common in alcohol withdrawal and can contribute to dysrhythmias.

Extended electrolytes (calcium, magnesium, and phosphate). Magnesium is often low in those who are dependent on alcohol. In addition, hypomagnesaemia is associated with severe withdrawal and puts them at increased risk of arrhythmias (Torsades de Pointes).

Creatinine. Creatinine measures kidney function and becomes elevated with kidney dysfunction.

Glucose. Low or high blood sugar levels can mimic intoxication or withdrawal states.

Hepatic transaminases (AST, ALT, GGT). An elevated GGT may indicate an alcohol consumption of usually more than four drinks per day. However, it is not a sensitive measure and a normal GGT does not rule out an alcohol problem. GGT usually rises and falls with alcohol use (the half-life is approximately four weeks), but it does not reflect recent changes to use. In alcoholic hepatitis, the user's AST is greater than ALT by a ratio of 2:1. In viral hepatitis, ALT is greater than AST.

Liver function tests (alkaline phosphatase, INR, and bilirubin). These tests should be ordered if there are any signs of chronic liver disease. High bilirubin and INR and low albumin indicate hepatic dysfunction.

Urine drug screen (UDS). UDS is a screening tool, but it cannot quantify the amount of drug used. There can be false positives and negatives, so one must be careful about assuming drug use with a positive result. If there is a serious consequence to a positive drug test (e.g., parole violation or suspension of driver's license), then ask the laboratory to do confirmatory testing. Detection of the substance is affected by how long ago the drug was taken, hepatic and renal clearance, protein binding, and the rate of drug metabolism.

Methamphetamine, amphetamine and MDMA can be detected within two to three days of use. Morphine (metabolite of heroin, codeine, and hydromorphone) is detectable within two to four days; however, the test cannot distinguish between opioids. Heroin cannot be detected via urine. PCP is detectable within two to three days, but not all centres routinely test for it in the urine and so it is necessary to specify that testing for PCP is required. Cocaine metabolite (benzoylecgonine) is detectable for three, sometimes five, days after use. The marijuana metabolite (Δ9-tetrahydrocannabinoic acid) is detectable in the UDS for days, sometimes weeks (if the individual is a chronic user) after use. Benzodiazepines can be detectable for up to days or weeks after use, depending on a particular drug's half-life. Alcohol is detectable via UDS, but a more useful test is the BAC. It can be detected in the urine for up to 12 hours.

BHCG for women of child-bearing age.   BHCG is a hormone released in increasing amounts during the initial stage of pregnancy. It is useful to check if the individual is pregnant because many substances especially alcohol can be harmful to the fetus. In addition, sudden withdrawal of opioids can cause miscarriages and other harmful effects for the woman. Often in early stages of pregnancy the individual may not be aware that they are pregnant and a positive BHCG will likely change your management. Usually opioid withdrawal is not life threatening. However, in pregnancy, due to the risk of miscarriage, consider a gradual withdrawal of opioids, or switch to methadone, which is safer than an abrupt discontinuation of the opioid.

ECG.   Cocaine or amphetamine intoxication, as well as alcohol and benzodiazepine intoxication and withdrawal can affect the heart. They can cause arrhythmias, and in individuals with chronic substance use, there can often be long-term damage detected via the ECG (cardiomyopathy, supraventricular and ventricular tachycardias, and LV dysfunction).

Hepatitis B and C, HIV, and sexually transmitted infections (STIs).   Those individuals who are alcohol dependent have a higher prevalence of hepatitis B and hepatitis C. Individuals who use IV drugs are particularly at risk for transmission of hepatitis B and C, as well as HIV. Often, when individuals are intoxicated or have blackouts, they are more susceptible to high-risk behaviours including unprotected sexual practices. It is important to ask the survivor's permission before administering the above STI, hepatitis and HIV testing. Hepatitis and HIV testing is indicated for everyone.

This is not intended to be an exhaustive list of investigations, but rather a quick screening list. If there are obvious signs of ill health and one or more of these tests are abnormal it likely warrants further investigation regarding both extent of drug use and any underlying medical conditions that may be a consequence of substance use or that may be exacerbated by substance use.

Abstinence Models and Harm Reduction Models

The abstinence model is based on the idea that once someone becomes dependent on a substance they have to completely abstain from that substance. Groups such as Alcoholics Anonymous and Narcotics Anonymous use the abstinence model. The harm-reduction model focuses on reducing substance use rather than complete discontinuation as the goal. The idea behind this model is that significantly reducing substance use is a lot easier than trying for complete abstinence, and will still be beneficial to the survivor.

Treat according to stage of change.   Regardless of the model with which one works, it is important to avoid coercing those with trauma histories to accept treatment, as this can make them less likely to seek care. Establish goals based on the survivor's stage (DiClemente & Prochaska, 1998). It is important to determine what stage the survivor is in so that the assessment and treatment can be tailored for them. The stages are described below.

Pre-contemplative stage.   When in the pre-contemplative stage, individuals do not usually attend treatment for substance use. This can be particularly true for individuals with trauma histories as the substance use may be a major coping strategy. Giving up the substance may mean a worsening in the re-experiencing symptoms associated with trauma or an overall lower level of functioning. The major task at this stage is to build the therapeutic relationship.

General guidelines for this stage include:

- General outreach (contract for care, be willing to provide follow-up appointments, and give contact information for additional resources).
- Focus on practical assistance (such as clothing or bus tickets).
- Stabilize symptoms (managing withdrawal, intoxication, and co-morbid illnesses).
- Enhance social networks and connectedness.
- Involve the family, if possible, and only if the survivor feels it would be therapeutic.
- Avoid legal penalties. Nevertheless, physicians have a duty to report around impaired driving and/or impairment in specific professions. Physicians do not have the authority to revoke or reinstate licenses, but can advocate on the survivor's behalf with the ministry of transport to show that the individual is seeking help.
- Closely monitor.

Contemplation stage.   Individuals who are in the contemplation stage may recognize the disadvantages of substance abuse and the benefits of changing, but they may feel ambivalent about giving up their substance use as a coping mechanism. Trauma survivors may be stuck in this stage for long periods of time, so maintaining engagement with the survivor despite their ambivalence is a crucial goal of the practitioner.

Preparation stage.   Individuals who are in the stage of preparation are getting ready to abstain from or reduce substance intake and may have made attempts to quit in the past. It is important for trauma survivors to recognize that there may be a worsening in other symptoms and to prepare themselves for any increase in symptoms that the substance use was helping them to avoid. Re-experiencing symptoms such as flashbacks or nightmares may become worse. The use of previously used avoidance strategies such as self-harm may seem like the only alternative to the survivor. An increase in affect dysregulation may occur if the survivor was using substances as a way to regulate their affect. Educating the survivor about what they can expect when they stop using the substances will create an opportunity to learn more positive coping strategies and alternate ways to regulate their affect. Not educating the individual sets them up for failure.

Consider substance use programs that are tailored to individuals with a history of trauma, inpatient settings with a focus on all aspects of trauma care, and individual counselors who can provide ongoing care for both the substance use and the history of trauma. Most major cities have a "clearinghouse" for addiction services. Get to know these resources and how to access them as they are an invaluable resource.

Consider applying some of the following interventions:

- Education may happen over the course of weeks and months rather than in a single session. Refer to self-care handouts, focus on building distress tolerance skills, and recognize that substance use may be a misused self-soothing strategy.
- Motivational interviewing skills can be used extensively during the preparation stage.
- Identify and try to address the survivor's perceived barriers to treatment. If residential treatment is not an option because of cost, consider accessing subsidized programs or going through their extended benefit plan at work.
- Encourage attendance at harm reduction or abstinence groups. AA or NA groups take place in most urban and rural areas. There are also a number of online groups for individuals who find it hard to attend meetings.
- Consider the use of medication for the following: symptom relief, help with substance cravings or to treat co-morbid illnesses that may affect their substance use.
- Prepare the survivor for a lifestyle change. Spending time with friends or engagement in social activities can often be centred on substance use. Perhaps they only see their friends when they drink together. Perhaps their friends encourage their use, either intentionally or unknowingly. Help the survivor navigate these social situations. Role-plays are a great tool for this as it is often hard for survivors to say "no" when offered a drink or a drug. Let them be the persistent friend and demonstrate what could be said in the situation to avoid substance use.

Action stage. Individuals who are in the action stage are focused on reducing or abstaining from substances. The main goal at this point is to help the survivor build belief in their abilities to reduce or abstain from substance use.

Consider using some of the following interventions:

- Help them develop problem-solving and coping skills.
- Suggest CBT and self-help groups (AA, NA).
- Use medication as an agonist substitution (see below) to decrease cravings or to reduce the reinforcing effects of substances.

Maintenance stage. Trauma survivors who are currently in the maintenance stage may benefit from learning additional strategies to help bolster their skills in avoiding substances. An excellent resource is *Seeking safety: A treatment manual for PTSD and substance abuse* (Najavits, 2002).

Consider applying some of the following interventions:

- Address lifestyle improvements such as furthering their education, looking at better job opportunities, or achieving a better work–life balance.
- If the survivor is not independently housed (e.g., is in a shelter), independent housing may be the next step in further stabilization.

Withdrawal Management

In this section, the focus is on benzodiazepine and alcohol withdrawal as these dependencies can be life threatening in the withdrawal phase. Cocaine withdrawal is largely psychological and management is mostly supportive. Benzodiazepines may be useful for agitation in other substance withdrawal states. If the individual did not previously experience mild complications with withdrawal, such as anxiety, insomnia, or mild tremor, they will likely not require pharmacotherapy or medical treatment. However, in the case of alcohol and benzodiazepine withdrawal, both of which can be life-threatening, a good history of current and past use as well as past withdrawal symptoms is essential to determining how to tailor care. It is also important to advise the user not to abruptly stop their alcohol or benzodiazepine use if the use has been prolonged, as they will risk experiencing life threatening withdrawal symptoms. Instead, plan treatment around a set stop date so that they can be managed in a medical setting if necessary.

Management of Uncomplicated Alcohol Withdrawal

Withdrawal management should ideally occur under medical supervision, in an outpatient setting or through a day treatment program. The CIWA-A (Clinical Institute Withdrawal Assessment for Alcohol) scale (Sullivan, Sykora, Schneiderman, Naranjo, & Sellers, 1989) is a valid and reliable instrument used in medical settings to manage alcohol withdrawal. It contains 10 items pertaining to the following: nausea and vomiting; agitation; anxiety; tremor; tactile, auditory and visual hallucinations; paroxysmal sweats; headache; and disorientation. Each item is scored from 0 to 7. Heart rate and blood pressure are also measured with each assessment. A total score of greater than 10 means that the person should be treated with benzodiazepines. The CIWA-A scale can be found online, but nurses and physicians have to be trained in implementing the scale. This scale is not meant to be used by non-medical practitioners.

The following are some additional recommendations for using the CIWA-A. Begin the CIWA-A protocol six to eight hours after the individual's last drink. If the CIWA-A score is greater than or equal to 10, load with diazepam 20mg po (by mouth) every one to two hours. A score of less than 10 on three consecutive readings indicates that withdrawal has been completed. If the person will be returning home that day, do not provide more than two to three tablets of 10mg diazepam PRN as take-home tablets. Caution must be used since there is a risk for life-threatening complications (e.g., severe respiratory depression) if the tablets are taken in conjunction with alcohol. Follow up the next day if possible. Treating withdrawal with take-home medications is generally not recommended unless the user is extremely reliable, has someone reliable at home who can provide some monitoring and assistance, and is not going to drink alcohol while on diazepam.

Management of Complicated Alcohol Withdrawal

If the user has a history of withdrawal seizures, dysrhythmias, hallucinations, or delirium, they must be managed in a hospital or medical detox setting. There is no need to describe complicated withdrawal exhaustively here as management of this type of withdrawal should not be conducted in an office setting.

Seizure prevention. Use diazepam 20mg q1–2hrs for a minimum of three doses. Continue if the CIWA-A score is greater than or equal to 10. Do not use antiepileptic medication unless the user has a seizure disorder or has had more than two seizures despite diazepam treatment. A medical work-up should be completed to investigate for other causative factors for the seizures (e.g., head injury and CNS infection).

If dysrhythmia is suspected. Use the usual diazepam management but also focus on correcting fluid or electrolyte imbalances. Treat dysrhythmia, and transfer the individual to the ER setting or inpatient setting where cardiac monitoring is accessible.

Withdrawal hallucinations. Use diazepam management for a minimum of three doses and in conjunction with seizure-lowering antipsychotics (such as risperidone) or an anti-epileptic medication such as valproic acid.

Withdrawal delirium. Use both diazepam and antipsychotics. Address any underlying medical illnesses (e.g., pneumonia). Treat this as a medical emergency as there is a 20% mortality rate associated with withdrawal delirium.

Note that lorazepam (sl/po, 1–2mg q2–4hrs for CIWA-A $\geq$ 10) should be used in place of diazepam for individuals with liver dysfunction, the elderly or individuals who are in respiratory distress. Diazepam has a longer half-life and is more taxing on the liver.

Benzodiazepine Withdrawal

If the user decides they are ready to stop using benzodiazepines, it is best to taper them gradually over weeks rather than abruptly stopping the medication because the withdrawal can be severe. Taper as an outpatient if the user is taking less than 50mg per day of diazepam equivalent or 50–100mg per day. They have to be both medically and psychiatrically stable and not dependent on other drugs. Use inpatient tapering if they are using more than 100mg per day of diazepam equivalent.

With outpatient tapering of benzodiazepines, first convert the benzodiazepine of use to a long-acting benzodiazepine, such as clonazepam or diazepam (resources such as the CPS (Compendium of pharmaceuticals and specialties) manual can be used to assist with conversion). Keep in mind the following as a benchmark:

0.25mg clonazepam = 0.5mg lorazepam = 5mg diazepam

The maximum amount of diazepam equivalents that should be used is 80–100mg per day in divided doses. Taper by 10% of the original dose every one to two weeks. Once the daily dose reaches 20% of the original dose, taper by 5% every two to four weeks. The tapering schedule may need to be modified slightly for each individual based on their withdrawal symptoms. Often, the hardest part of the taper for the user in terms of withdrawal symptoms or rebound symptoms is the last 10% of the medication.

When completing an inpatient taper, start the taper at half or one-third of the equivalent diazepam dose and administer the medication divided into TID or QID dosing (three or four times per day). If it is not well tolerated the dose can be increased by 20–30mg of diazepam and continue the taper. Occasional prn doses during the taper can be given if needed. They must be monitored closely for sedation or respiratory depression. Try not to reduce the dose by more than 10% of the daily dose every day, and reduce the frequency of dose reduction as the dose decreases.

Opioid Withdrawal

There are no serious complications with opioid withdrawal for the healthy, non-pregnant individual. However, suicidal ideation may become an issue secondary to the anxiety and dysphoria that follows withdrawal. Spontaneous abortion and pre-term labor are risks for the pregnant woman who goes into withdrawal. Individuals need to be warned about the loss of tolerance within three to seven days of discontinuing opioids and the risk of overdose.

Clonidine, although less effective than methadone in managing withdrawal, is more readily accessible, and any physician can prescribe it. Clonidine can cause postural hypotension and should be used with caution and only after a medical history, physical, and a medication review have been completed. Antinauseants, antidiarrheal and analgesic medications can be used to make the individual more comfortable during withdrawal. Analgesics and sedative medications can also be helpful for muscle aches and insomnia, respectively. Methadone treatment can only be accessed through a licensed clinic, where specialist physicians prescribe the medication. This may be a good option and should be explored fully.

Pharmacotherapy Options for Substance Dependence

The following are some medication options for individuals with substance dependence who need additional help managing cravings while trying to reduce or abstain from substances. This section is meant to act as an overview of the possible medication options. These medications should only be prescribed by a physician who is familiar with them and can provide close monitoring.

Alcohol Reduction

There are two medications that can help manage cravings for alcohol: acamprosate and naltrexone. Over time, with chronic alcohol use, there is an increase in glutamate, an excitatory neuron. The increase in glutamate ultimately leads to alcohol cravings. Acamprosate acts by reducing the surge of glutamate that occurs when alcohol is consumed.

Naltrexone is a competitive opioid antagonist, and blocks the effects of endorphins that are released when someone consumes alcohol, therefore reducing the pleasurable effects of alcohol consumption. It has to be used with caution as it can cause hepatotoxicity and needs to be monitored closely.

Disulfiram, or antabuse, is a medication that works by inhibiting acetaldehyde dehydrogenase, which causes a toxic build-up of acetaldehyde when someone uses alcohol. Using alcohol while on disulfiram often results in flushed face, vomiting, headache, chest pain, palpitations and, in serious cases, seizure or hypotension. It is considered an aversive therapy and should only be used for those who can take disulfiram under the daily supervision of a spouse, partner or a pharmacist.

Opioid Reduction

Naltrexone can also help manage cravings caused by the reduction of, or abstinence from, opioids. A dose of naltrexone can completely block the effects of opioids for up to 72 hours; therefore, it is pointless for the individual to use an opioid during that time as they get no effect.

Methadone is an opioid and can only be prescribed by physicians who have a special exemption. It is a highly effective treatment for opioid dependence, can reduce injection drug use, and can help people lead more productive lives. Methadone use is intended to reduce drug cravings and withdrawal symptoms.

Buprenorphine is a μ-opioid receptor partial agonist and a kappa opioid receptor antagonist. It acts similarly to methadone in reducing withdrawal symptoms and illicit opioid use. It has a much lower risk of death in overdose compared with methadone and only takes days to titrate to the optimal dose compared with methadone, which can take weeks.

Nicotine Reduction

Nicotine replacement therapies like the nicotine patch, inhalers, and gum are readily available and can be prescribed by any physician—and in some areas, by pharmacists. They are also often covered by drug benefit plans.

Bupropion is an antidepressant that blocks the reuptake of dopamine and norepinephrine and reduces cravings and withdrawal symptoms. It is best to start it at least 10 days to two weeks before the "quit date" and is usually maintained for three months or longer.

Varenicline, or Champix, is a nicotine receptor partial agonist and reduces cravings and withdrawal symptoms.

Psychotherapies Useful in Substance Use Disorders

Once a thorough assessment has been completed and intoxication and withdrawal symptoms that may be affecting the current presentation have been recognized, the next step is treatment initiation. There are a number of therapies designed for treatment of substance use disorders and individual anxiety and mood disorders. However, effective treatments target both the substance use disorder and the mood or anxiety disorder. A coordinated form of treatment usually means a better outcome for individuals (Mills et al., 2012). With respect to PTSD and substance use disorders, there is evidence to support significant improvements in both the anxiety symptoms and the substance use (Back et al., 2012).

Therapies Developed for Addiction Disorders

Motivational Interviewing (MI) and Motivational Enhancement Therapy (MET). MET is the longer-term follow-up to an initial brief intervention strategy. It continues the use of motivational interviewing and moves an individual closer to a readiness to change substance use behaviours. It was initially developed by William Miller and Stephen Rollnick (2002). It combines techniques from cognitive, client-centred, systems, and social-psychological persuasion approaches and may be provided by trained clinicians in substance abuse facilities, mental health clinics, and private practice offices (APA Practice Guidelines, 2006).

Therapies Adapted for Use with Addiction Disorders

Integrated cognitive behavioural therapy (CBT). This is a brief, manualized psychotherapy that was originally designed to treat depression. Cognitive–behavioural strategies are based on the theory that learning processes play a critical role in the development of maladaptive behaviour patterns. Individuals learn to identify and correct problematic behaviours (CANMAT, 2009). Integrated CBT combines cognitive and behavioural interventions for both anxiety disorders and co-occurring substance use disorders (Back, 2010).

Seeking safety. This is also a manualized, integrative group CBT. It was specifically designed to treat individuals struggling with co-occurring PTSD and substance use. The focus is on a combination of education and coping skills (Najavits, 2002).

Supportive expressive therapy. This is a brief model of psychodynamic psychotherapy including both supportive and expressive interventions (Leichsenring & Leibing, 2007).

Interpersonal psychotherapy. Interpersonal psychotherapy is a brief, manualized, dynamically-informed psychotherapy (Klerman, Weissman, Rounsaville, & Chevron, 1984). It explores the connection between interpersonal interactions and mental illness. It aims to improve interpersonal functioning, and deal with the social consequences of substance use (Weissman, Markowitz, & Klerman, 2000).

Conclusion

Substance use often becomes a coping mechanism for trauma survivors, but what starts as an escape may quickly evolve into another major health consequence. It is imperative to explore substance use initially and in follow up sessions as it has such a major impact on the survivor's level of functioning, ability to learn good coping mechanisms, and their health.

Gathering a clear and detailed history is the first step. Education around the impact of substance use on their lives and their ability to cope is the next step. Learning and substituting better coping skills—described in the other chapters— in place of substance use is the goal.

Questions to Think About

1. Sophia presents for help after being beaten up outside of a bar. The clinician discovers that Sophia has struggled with addiction for the past 12 years.

Following this assault, she has been drinking most days. A non-trauma-informed approach may focus strictly on stabilization as the goal and encourage an abstinence program. How would a trauma-informed approach inform your understanding of Sophia? What would be the focus of a trauma-informed approach in this situation?

2. Natasha is a 26-year-old woman with a history of extensive childhood trauma. She is presenting in the emergency room in an acute crisis following the loss of her job and is at-risk of losing her housing. She is intoxicated on alcohol at the time. You see her in your office a few days later and she describes significant (three times per week) episodes of binge drinking, causing her to miss work and leading to the loss of her job. Natasha does not believe that her drinking is a concern. Although she is able to identify that there have been consequences to her alcohol use, she wishes to focus only on her trauma history and job loss at this time. What are your thoughts about engaging in any form of trauma-focused treatment given her substance use?

3. What concerns might you have if a survivor with alcohol dependency issues suddenly stops drinking?

10

A TRAUMA-INFORMED
APPROACH TO MEDICATIONS

This chapter provides a trauma-informed approach to medication when necessary in a survivor's treatment plan. It is written for physicians who may be providing care and prescribing medications in a mental health or healthcare setting. However, it is important for all providers working as part of a multi-disciplinary team to understand whether or not medication is a good option for a survivor and to know how to support them during treatment.

The information provided in this chapter is not to be used as a standard treatment for every survivor who presents with symptoms of PTSD or complex trauma. Medication decisions should be made based on the needs of each individual and not solely because they happen to have a cluster of symptoms. Much of the current literature focuses on patients who meet criteria for PTSD or other disorders according to the DSM-IV. In order to be consistent with the evidence base in the medical literature, medications are reviewed based on the "disorders" they were designed to treat. Clinically, however, many survivors with complex trauma do not fit neatly into diagnostic categories, yet their lives are profoundly affected and many of their symptoms can be alleviated with the use of medication. Judicious use of medication for survivors who do not meet criteria is still useful and can help the survivor towards recovery. Most importantly, all medication suggestions should only be prescribed by a qualified physician and be reviewed in detail with the individual prior to the start of treatment.

General Guidelines

The mainstay of PTSD treatment in a clinical setting is a combination of anti-depressant medication and cognitive behavioural therapy (Hetrick, Purcell, Garner, & Parslow, 2010). Ideally, treatment is initiated shortly after the diagnosis has been made; that is to say, it begins within four weeks of the traumatic event occurring and progression to PTSD. In reality, survivors with PTSD often present to treatment months or even years later. They may have gone on to develop co-morbid substance use disorders, dissociative disorders, eating disorders, or somatoform disorders as coping mechanisms. Their history of trauma may predispose them to developing a mood disorder such as major depressive disorder (MDD) or may unmask an underlying bipolar spectrum disorder. Anxiety disorders, such as panic disorder, social phobia, or generalized anxiety symptoms, commonly occur in individuals with extensive trauma histories and will affect not only their ability to access care, but also the severity of their trauma symptoms and overall level of functioning. Thus, as the care provider, it is important to address not only the use of medication to manage specific symptoms of PTSD, but also to consider the role of medications in managing co-morbid medical and psychiatric illnesses.

Through a full psychiatric assessment, the provider can determine which symptom clusters are present, whether or not the survivor meets criteria for PTSD, and if any co-morbid disorders are complicating the clinical picture. The next steps are to determine treatment priorities, determine which symptoms will respond to medications, avoid polypharmacy, identify the goals and rationale with the survivor, and educate the survivor about the medication.

Determine Treatment Priorities

When a survivor presents with PTSD but also struggles with co-morbid illnesses, the provider must determine where to focus medication treatment. It is important to remember that safety is always the priority. Once safety has been established, the provider can focus on treating other symptoms. For example, if a survivor is acutely suicidal and depressed but also has symptoms of somatization, it would make sense to prioritize the survivor's safety and address the major depressive episode rather than focusing at the outset on the somatoform disorder.

Not All Symptoms Respond to Medications

Certain symptoms that present in the context of a trauma history are more responsive to psychotherapy interventions, while others may respond more favourably to pharmacotherapy. Medications have been useful in reducing symptoms such as hyperarousal and mood symptoms, but tend to be less effective for symptoms like dissociation (Ravindran & Stein, 2009b). Dissociation is the result of limited affect regulation capabilities and may be best addressed with skill development rather than specific medications. Sleep disruption may require attention to sleep hygiene and the use of specific medications, especially in the short-term. Not attending to sleep with medication may limit the survivor's ability to learn or implement skills that they are working on in therapy.

Avoid Polypharmacy

The provider needs to consider the entirety of the survivor's clinical picture and should aim to target as many symptoms as possible with the fewest possible medications. This aim is often quite attainable because a single medication, when carefully selected, can be used to address multiple concerns. For example, SSRIs work to treat PTSD, MDD, and anxiety disorders, as well as impulsivity and symptoms of aggression.

Once the provider has determined that the survivor requires medication as part of their treatment plan, the provider should identify the goals of the proposed treatment, have a clear rationale for the treatment plan and empower the survivor by educating them on what to expect with the medication.

Identify Goals

For survivors who present in crisis, clinicians should consider using medication for the purpose of stabilizing symptoms. Medications are useful in reducing re-experiencing symptoms of PTSD and reducing hyperarousal. Medications are less useful in reducing avoidance behaviours or emotional numbing. If the survivor struggles with co-morbid illnesses that are significant enough to interfere with daily functioning and are contributing to the crisis, then those too need to be addressed with medication when appropriate. A substance use disorder is an example of a co-morbid illness that may also respond to medication management.

Symptoms may not always technically meet criteria for a DSM-5 diagnosis, but they may still impair the survivor's functioning or their ability to engage in treatment. Not every survivor who is functionally impaired by their trauma histories will necessarily meet criteria for PTSD, but their functioning may still be profoundly impaired and medication should still be considered.

Have a Clear Rationale for a Medication Plan

Before starting any medication, the provider should have a clear rationale for their medication choices, identify the specific symptoms being targeted and identify both short-term and long-term outcome measures. This will make it much easier to monitor the success of the medication in treating the survivor's symptoms. The outcomes chosen for monitoring must be specific and related to functioning, so as to be relevant to the survivor. Be clear with the survivor about the rationale for the proposed treatment.

Empower and Educate Survivors

It is the provider's responsibility to educate and empower survivors by making them aware of the treatment rationale and creating a therapeutic space that is safe enough for them to openly discuss feelings around adherence. Survivors with trauma histories may be particularly sensitive to feelings of loss of control, so it is essential to empower survivors and to help put the control back in their hands. This is accomplished by giving the survivor as much choice as possible about which medication to use, explaining the rationale for each medication option and being as flexible as possible with the initiation of the medication.

Recommended Areas of Medication Treatment

A combination of psychotherapy and pharmacotherapy is preferred by most prescribing providers. For PTSD symptoms, much of the current literature and evidence is based on the DSM-IV criteria for PTSD, which had three symptom clusters: intrusive symptoms, avoidance, and hyperarousal. However, the new "fourth cluster" in the DSM-5 (American Psychiatric Association, 2013) includes many of the symptoms that were previously listed in "avoidance." Below is a discussion of medication treatment for the particular areas of difficulty often experienced by survivors. These include: PTSD symptoms (intrusion symptoms, avoidance, negative alterations in cognitions and mood, and hyperarousal); anxiety symptoms and major depressive disorder symptoms; self-harm, aggression, and impulsivity; insomnia; and substance use concerns. (See Chapter 9 for a discussion of substance use.)

PTSD symptoms

It is important to remember that many survivors who seek mental health or healthcare support have not yet met criteria for PTSD because their traumatic event occurred less than one month ago. These survivors, however, may meet criteria for acute stress disorder. (See Chapter 2 for DSM-5 criteria.)

Selective serotonin reuptake inhibitors (SSRIs) are considered a first-line treatment for the symptoms of PTSD (Stein, Ipser, & Seedat, 2006). Although the provider should start the medication titration at the low end of the dose range, it is recommended that the dose be increased to the higher end of the therapeutic range and maintained on the highest dose the individual can tolerate for at least six to eight weeks to consider the trial adequate.

Serotonin–norepinephrine reuptake inhibitors (SNRIs) are also useful in the treatment of PTSD symptoms, but there is less robust evidence to support their use compared with the evidence for SSRIs.

There is mixed evidence from clinical trials to support atypical antipsychotics such as risperidone and olanzapine as adjunctive treatments. The atypical antipsychotics as additions to SSRIs or SNRIs may be useful in reducing re-experiencing and hyperarousal symptoms. Alpha-adrenergic receptor blockers have been shown to be useful in reducing nightmares and improving sleep, and they have been shown in small trials to be helpful in reducing nightmares and improving sleep

(Raskind et al., 2003). Doses of medication used for PTSD are similar to those recommended for other psychiatric diagnoses (APA Practice Guidelines, 2004).

Symptoms of Major Depression and Anxiety

Major depression and depressive symptoms are commonly co-morbid with PTSD. Luckily, both classes of first-line medications for PTSD are also first-line medications for those who meet criteria for moderate to severe MDD. SSRIs, Venlafaxine (an SNRI), and Wellbutrin are considered first-line antidepressants in the treatment of major depression. Tricyclic antidepressants (TCAs) and trazodone are recommended second-line antidepressants because of tolerability and safety issues. MAOIs are considered third-line antidepressants because they necessitate dietary restrictions and because they interact with multiple drugs (Yatham et al., 2009).

Although there are a number of different anxiety disorders, each anxiety disorder may require its own specific psychotherapeutic approach to treatment. Almost all anxiety disorders can be treated with antidepressant medication in combination with psychotherapy. Benzodiazepines can provide short-term relief. The provider may wish to consider using benzodiazepines as a short-term adjunct to antidepressant medication. Antidepressant medications typically take six weeks or longer to reduce anxiety symptoms. Therefore, for symptomatic relief, benzodiazepines can be of assistance with acute anxiety. Consider minimizing benzodiazepine use in panic disorder as it may reinforce avoidance behaviour and worsen panic symptoms. There is a potential for dependence to develop for benzodiazepines if they are used long-term, especially for survivors with a history of problems with substance use.

Impulsivity, Aggression and Self-Injurious Behaviour

In order to address impulsivity, aggression, and self-injurious behaviour, the provider has few options. The use of medications such as topiramate or lamotrigine is a novel approach for anger control and is supported by some evidence. For PTSD specifically, topiramate has only mixed evidence (Lindley, Carlson, & Hill, 2007). There is good evidence supporting the use of SSRIs in the management of these symptoms (APA Practice Guidelines, 2001). SSRIs help in controlling these symptoms and their benefit is independent and in addition to their effect on mood symptoms. They should be considered for first-line use.

Neuroleptics or atypical antipsychotics are increasingly used as adjunctive medication or even used alone for impulsivity or aggression. Consequently, the provider may consider the addition of a low dose neuroleptic (atypical antipsychotic) to the SSRI. Caution must be taken due to the problematic side effect profile (sedation, weight gain, orthostatic hypotension) of these drugs.

Mood stabilizers, such as lithium, valproic acid, and carbamazapine, can be used as primary treatment or as adjunctive treatment. However, their side-effect profile can be extensive and they have multiple medication interactions. This is especially true of carbamazepine which interacts with multiple medications (APA Practice Guidelines, 2001).

Insomnia

Sleep is often severely disrupted in trauma survivors. Insomnia may be secondary to the hypervigilance or re-experiencing symptoms of PTSD, or it may be a manifestation of heightened anxiety, substance use, substance withdrawal or depression. Some survivors' trauma occurred at nighttime, and this may cause an exacerbation of symptoms at night and worsen their insomnia.

Regardless of the underlying issue, it is important to gather a detailed sleep history and consider having the survivor keep a sleep journal prior to an appointment. There are a number of downloadable sleep-charts or sleep-logs that can be given to the survivor to complete.

Detailed sleep history. Before resorting to medication as a solution to the survivor's sleep difficulties, it is important to gather a detailed sleep history. If the sleep difficulty is related to poor sleep hygiene, it may be possible to avoid using medications altogether. The following information should be gathered:

- Is this a chronic or recent issue?
  - o Does the sleep disturbance predate the trauma?
  - o Were there any identifiable stressors at the time of the sleep disturbance?
  - o How problematic do they find the insomnia?
- What are the main sleep complaints?
  - o Do they have trouble falling asleep (initial insomnia)?
  - o Do they have problems staying asleep (middle insomnia)?
  - o Do they wake up too early (late insomnia)?
  - o Are they able to fall back asleep if they wake up?
  - o How many hours do they sleep?
  - o What is the quality of their sleep?
  - o Do they have vivid dreams or nightmares that disrupt sleep?
  - o Are they restless during sleep?
  - o Do they feel tired after they awaken?
  - o Do they experience excessive daytime sedation?
  - o Does their partner note restlessness during sleep?
  - o Does their partner note disruptions in breathing during sleep?
- What is their usual sleep routine?
  - o What time do they usually get to bed?
  - o How much time do they spend awake in bed?
  - o Do they watch TV or use the computer right before trying to fall asleep?
  - o Do they nap during the day?

- What is their sleep environment?
  - o Do they have a TV or computer in their bedroom?
  - o Is there noise when they are trying to sleep?
  - o Is there light in their bedroom?
- What is their method of waking?
  - o Do they use alarms?
  - o Do they awaken naturally?
  - o Does their partner awaken them?
- What is their typical daily routine?
  - o Do they work shift work?
  - o What time is their last meal of the day?
  - o Do they eat sugary food late at night?
  - o Are they doing any exercise at night?
- What are the timing and quantities of substances consumed in a day or week?
  - o How much alcohol do they use daily?
  - o How much caffeine do they have in a day (including coffee, tea, soda or energy drinks)?
  - o When is their last caffeine intake of the day?
  - o Do they smoke cigarettes?
  - o Do they use any street drugs? If so, which one(s) and how much?
  - o Do they use any street drugs to help them sleep?
  - o What regular medication are they on?
  - o Do they ever use over-the-counter medications to help them fall asleep? If they do, which medication, what dosage, what time is it taken?

Sleep hygiene.   Prior to considering medication, the provider should address any issues of poor sleep hygiene. It is important to note that poor sleep hygiene may be a result of lack of self-care. (Refer to Chapter 8 for more information on self-care.) The following is a list of suggestions the provider can share with the survivor about what constitutes good "sleep hygiene":

- Establish a regular bedtime routine;
- Establish a regular waking time each day, and maintain it on days off;
- Reduce noise or light in the bedroom;
- Avoid television or the computer at least an hour before sleep;
- Avoid having a television or computer in the bedroom;
- Create a proper sleep environment and maintain comfortable sleeping conditions;
- Practice evening relaxation routines, such as progressive muscle relaxation or meditation;
- Avoid napping during the day, except when a sleep chart shows that the naps induce better sleep at nighttime;
- Avoid caffeinated beverages after 4:00 PM. Caffeine intake should stop after 2:00 PM or noon if someone is sensitive to the effects;

- Reduce smoking, especially late in the evening;
- Reduce or terminate use of nicotine, excessive alcohol, stimulants or long-term use of benzodiazepines as they can profoundly disrupt sleep initiation and the sleep cycle;
- Exercise regularly during the day. A graded program of vigorous exercise is helpful, but avoid late evening exercise as it can interfere with sleep;
- Limit daily "in-bed time" to the usual amount present before the sleep disturbance. Example: avoid staying in bed for hours, hoping to fall back asleep in the early morning;
- Try very hot, 20-minute, body temperature-raising bath soaks near bedtime;
- Eat at regular times daily and avoid large meals near bedtime.

Drug treatments for insomnia.   Sometimes, sleep hygiene is not enough to treat insomnia. If this is the case, the provider can consider medication as an adjunct to good sleep hygiene. Some sleep difficulties of trauma survivors may resolve once symptoms of re-experiencing, anxiety, or hyperarousal improve. However, as mentioned earlier, there is often a delay between the advent of antidepressant treatment and the reduction in symptoms, even as long as six weeks. In the short term, additional sleep medications may need to be employed until the antidepressant medication can take effect. Ideally, benzodiazepines would not be used long-term because of the risk of dependence. It is also essential to review all the medications (prescription or non-prescription) that the trauma survivor is using before starting a sleep medication due to the risk of medication interactions.

If a decision is made to use a benzodiazepine, consider lorazepam, as it is shorter-acting. However, this also means that it has a higher potential for dependence to form. Therefore, it should be used only in the short term. Choose lorazepam, oxazepam, or temazepam for survivors who are elderly or have medical illnesses affecting their liver function. These three medications have a shorter half-life. Also, they undergo conjugation, not oxidation, by the liver for metabolism and are therefore less taxing on the liver. Consider using clonazepam if the survivor has both initial and middle-of-the-night insomnia. Clonazepam is longer acting, and therefore more helpful than lorazepam in assisting the survivor to stay asleep. With benzodiazepines, dose-related side effects such as drowsiness, fatigue, unsteadiness, lightheadedness, confusion, and anterograde amnesia may occur. These side effects should be discussed with the survivor prior to prescribing these medications. Survivors also have to use caution when driving and operating machinery while on these medications. Assess for daytime drowsiness, fall risk, over-sedation, and dependence and withdrawal symptoms while the survivor remains on these medications. All benzodiazepines can be potentially misused or abused, but of particular concern are diazepam, alprazolam, and triazolam.

Zopiclone, trazodone, mirtazapine, TCAs, atypical antipsychotics, and melatonin are more appropriate than benzodiazepines for longer-term use. Zopiclone acts by increasing the inhibitory action of GABA and increasing chloride conductance.

The initial dosing schedule is 3.75–15mg at bedtime and does not usually go higher than 15mg at bedtime. It starts working in approximately 30 minutes, but it tends to last 3.5–6.5 hours, so for many individuals it is only useful for sleep initiation rather than maintenance of sleep. Survivors who are using it occasionally for sleep maintenance can take an additional half dose if they wake during the night. A bitter metallic taste is a common side effect.

Trazodone is a serotonin-2 antagonist and serotonin reuptake inhibitor, and it is used as an antidepressant at doses between 150–400mg. At low doses, it is used specifically for sedation, but this is an off-label use and there is only limited data to support dosing for insomnia. The initial doses of trazodone that are used for sedation start at 25–50mg at bedtime, but the dose can be increased to 50–100mg at bedtime as necessary. Providers must also consider interactions with other medications, especially other antidepressants.

Mirtazapine is a noradrenergic and specific serotonergic agent as well as an alpha receptor antagonist. Like trazodone it is also an antidepressant medication. The dosage range is 15–45mg at bedtime for antidepressant effect. Lower dosing, in the 15–30mg range, is often more sedating than higher dosing. Mirtazapine as a sleeping medication is also considered an off-label use.

Amitriptyline, clomiprimine, and imipramine are examples of TCAs. Their use to treat insomnia is largely off-label. They should only be used at low doses, unless they are also being used to treat depression. Use caution when prescribing these medications as they can be lethal in overdose. The side effects of these medications often prohibit their use. Concerning side effects related to their cardiovascular and anticholinergic effect as well as their lowering of seizure threshold requires them to be used with caution.

Caution should be used with antidepressants in general for treating insomnia, as they tend to result in carry-over daytime sedation. TCAs in particular may interact with multiple classes of medications and a survivor's complete list of prescribed and over-the-counter medications needs to be reviewed prior to starting these medications.

Atypical antipsychotics such as quetiapine are often used to improve sleep. Consider using atypical antipsychotics only in cases of insomnia in the context of severe psychiatric illness. Use caution because of their side effect profile. Specifically, metabolic side effects, weight gain, and orthostatic hypotension can be problematic. Dosing in the treatment of insomnia is uncertain and there is limited evidence to support their use for this purpose.

Melatonin, which acts by initiating sleep, is generally helpful for circadian rhythm sleep disorders such as sleep disruption secondary to shift work. Doses start at 0.3–5mg at bedtime. However, individuals can use 6–9mg at bedtime. Melatonin is available over-the-counter.

Clonidine is also a reasonable option to reduce sleep disruption in PTSD. Clonidine is a centrally-acting alpha agonist which was developed to prevent hypertension, but it also has a number of other medical uses.

There is one small clinical study indicating that nabilone may assist in reducing the experience of nightmares and disruptive sleep in individuals with PTSD (Fraser, 2009). Nabilone is an endocannabinoid receptor agonist. Dosages range from 0.25mg daily to a maximum of 6mg daily, taken usually one hour prior to sleep. Common side effects include dizziness, lightheadedness, memory difficulties, and headache. However, the body of evidence supporting this as a first- or second-line option is not available as of yet and further studies are needed.

Encouraging Initiation of and Adherence to Treatment

Strategies to Support the Initiation of Medication Treatment

Taking medications may be a sensitive issue for trauma survivors for any number of reasons. It is essential to explore potential difficulties that the survivor may have with taking medications. The absence of a full discussion may risk eroding the therapeutic relationship and push the survivor not only to reject medication treatment, but may contribute to them feeling increasingly isolated and disconnected from accessing *any* treatment for symptoms of their trauma. It is also the prescribing physician's responsibility to gain informed consent about the medication that the survivor will be using.

When treating symptoms of PTSD or other trauma-related disorders with medication, there may be a number of barriers that impede the survivor's willingness to consider taking psychotropic medications. The survivor may view taking medication as a loss of control over their body and as disempowering, which are feelings that survivors have likely experienced in relation to their trauma. The survivor may be concerned about being drugged, which may also be related to previous traumatic experiences. It is not uncommon to hear individuals describe taking medications as a "sign of weakness." Strongly suggesting medication on the part of the prescriber may feel like coercion to the survivor, which may be experienced by the survivor as similar to previous trauma. For all of these reasons, it is important to address the survivor's concerns and to make the process of choosing and starting a medication as collaborative as possible.

Explore the survivor's previous experiences with medication, including what they liked about the medication and what did not work. In order to make the process of choosing and starting a medication as collaborative as possible it is important to effectively address any preconceived notions and worries about side effects. Encourage the survivor to ask questions.

When discussing medication options and when prescribing medication, provide as much information as possible. Provide both the generic name and the brand name. Give the rationale prescribing the medication. Explain the starting dose and target dose of the medication. Explain the delay that may occur between starting the medication and reduction in symptoms. Describe the likely duration of treatment and the possible side effects, both common and serious. Describe the monitoring strategies and early warning signs of drug toxicity. If there are alternatives to medication, they should also be described. Repeat instructions in different ways and at different times. Whenever possible, provide written instructions. Remember that the provider can write specific instructions on the prescription that will be transcribed onto the medication packaging by the pharmacist. Consider the overdose potential of the medication, especially before prescribing it to someone who is suicidal.

Adherence Considerations

There are a number of factors that predict non-adherence to medication. These include living alone or if the medication is unsupervised. Numerous unpleasant side effects from the medication can cause someone to not adhere. A complicated treatment regimen (three or more doses per day) or long-term treatment is associated with nonadherence. Most individuals struggle to complete a 14-day course of antibiotics, yet providers routinely ask individuals to take medications for months, sometimes years at a time. A previous history of non-adherence is another predictor. If an individual has found it difficult or is unwilling to take medications in the past it often speaks to their ambivalence around medication or lack of response to the treatment. Finally, costs associated with treatment will impact adherence.

There are a number of strategies the provider can use to enhance the survivor's adherence to medication. There are a number of ways to mitigate any adherence problems due to forgetfulness. These include minimizing the number of doses per day and using a long-acting formula whenever possible. The survivor can also be encouraged to link the medication administration with daily activities, for example, when brushing teeth or combing one's hair. They can set an alarm or create reminder notes. Using a dosette or having the pharmacy create medication blister packs can be helpful. Blister packs often make it easier for individuals to ensure they are taking the medication as prescribed, and it is already split up into daily doses.

If adherence problems are due to medication costs try switching or starting with a generic formulation of the medication. This can significantly reduce the cost. Explore government assistance plans. If the survivor is on social assistance or disability, explore their eligibility for provincial drug benefit plans.

Common Questions and Concerns of Trauma Survivors

Will Medication Change Personality?

It is not uncommon for someone prescribed psychotropic medication to say, "I don't want the medication to change who I am." It is helpful to reassure the survivor that medication cannot take away personality traits. The goal is to lower the "volume" on their symptoms so that they can better utilize therapy. The objective is to get the medication to facilitate learning and implementation of therapy skills.

Why Is Medication Necessary?

A survivor might ask, "Why do I need to take medication? That's not what I want to focus on." It is important to provide education about the illness, their symptoms and treatment. Providers should be prepared to go through their assessment and identify what made them decide on the diagnosis and treatment. Check in with the survivor regarding their understanding of the situation. Identify the survivor's fears and beliefs and address them thoroughly. Ask the survivor to communicate, in their own words, their understanding of what has been said by the provider.

Often, survivors have a belief that all they need is to "get it out, tell my story" in order to heal. In these cases, medication may be seen as numbing the feelings that the survivor wants to express and access. Reviewing stages of trauma treatment therapy may be helpful in these cases.

Consider saying the following to the survivor: "I understand that because you have been deeply traumatized you want to go deeply into your feelings in order to heal. It seems to make sense. But what we know from research is that if you go too deep too fast you risk retraumatizing yourself, which is not helpful. Research and our experience with many clients have shown that pacing and going slowly is the fastest way to heal. The decision about whether you take medication is always up to you. It's your body and your health and I would never suggest that you take this medication if you didn't want to. The reason I think it would be a good idea to give the medication a trial is so that we can try and improve your quality of life, stabilize your mood, and help you to better manage your symptoms. If over the course of giving this medication a good trial you decide you don't want to continue, I'll help you discontinue the medication, and if you are having difficulties with side effects then there are things we can do to manage the side effects. I'm really glad you brought this up and if you have any concerns it would be really important to discuss them openly as we are doing now."

Duration of Medication Treatment

Survivors may express a concern about never getting off medication, saying, "I don't want to be on medication for life!" This concern needs to be addressed based on the clinical history of the survivor. The prescribing provider will make different recommendations about duration of treatment depending on the survivor's specific set of circumstances and stage of treatment. For example, in the case of depression, there are certain circumstances in which a survivor would be advised to consider long-term to lifelong treatment, such as in the case of recurrent moderate-to-severe episodes of depression (Yatham et al., 2009).

During the acute phase of treating depression, the provider should advise the survivor to stay on the medication for up to a year (a minimum of six months past the point of remission), and even longer for anxiety disorders. If the survivor wishes to stop the medication early, which is ultimately the survivor's decision, it is best to do so slowly (over weeks) with the help of a physician to monitor discontinuation symptoms. If the survivor chooses to discontinue any medication, it is important for the provider to be vigilant about a recurrence of the survivor's mood and anxiety symptoms. Mood scales are useful tools for the survivor to monitor their mood, sleep, and anxiety symptoms daily. Mood charts and scales can also give the provider a more accurate sense of how the survivor is doing in between sessions, rather than relying solely on their memory during each session. A number of mood scales and charts are available online for no cost.

Side Effects

An understandable concern is about side effects. A survivor might say, "I've heard these medications have terrible side effects." Every medication has associated side effects. It is important to cover some of the common and rare-but-serious side effects. Consider giving the survivor a drug information handout and review it together. Remind them that not everyone gets every side effect and that many side effects will improve over time.

It is useful to explore what the survivor has heard about the medication. Do they know people who have taken it? From where did they get their information about the medication? Is it from a reputable source? Providers should be sure to direct them to reputable publications or websites.

A good general strategy for providers who are prescribing medications is to begin by exploring the survivor's concerns about side effects and addressing those concerns as thoroughly as possible. When the medication is begun, start low and go slow. Use an even lower starting dose than the published starting dose if the individual describes being sensitive to medications. Increase the dose gradually based on an assessment of the individual's response and the effectiveness of the medication. It may be appropriate to choose an alternate dosing schedule or use compounded doses. For example, moving a medication dose at nighttime can alleviate the concern of sedation as a side effect. The provider may also choose to split a dose into twice-a-day or three-times-a-day administration to improve tolerability for the individual. Create compounded dosing for individuals who have intolerable side effects even at starting doses. For example, the provider could try a compounded dose of venlafaxine at 15mg daily instead of 37.5mg daily (37.5mg daily is the lowest formulated dose available commercially). There are often a number of compounding pharmacies in most cities and there are Internet pharmacies that can provide this service. However, this option may be more expensive and the provider would need to ensure that it is either affordable for the individual or covered by their drug plan.

There are a number of strategies that can be used to problem-solve around common side effects. Below are a list of side effects and management strategies. The list of side effects is not meant to be comprehensive but rather act as a general guide. The prescribing provider will still need to go over the serious as well as the common side effects of each medication prescribed.

Headache. Headache can occur with the start of antidepressants and tends to be temporary (less than two weeks). Individuals suffering from this can use analgesics such as Tylenol or ibuprofen, as required.

Dry mouth. Dry mouth can occur with the use of antidepressants, mood stabilizers, and some antipsychotic medications. Sugarless sour candy or gum and sips of water during the day usually help to alleviate this symptom. Brushing or flossing one's teeth three to four times per day also helps.

Nausea and heartburn. To avoid nausea or heartburn, ask the individual to take the medication with food or at the end of a meal.

Drowsiness. Drowsiness associated with antidepressant use decreases somewhat with time. However, it can remain relatively stable with antipsychotics or mood stabilizers. Consider taking the medication close to bedtime and using the side effect as a sleep aid.

Dizziness. This is likely secondary to orthostatic hypotension. Orthostatic hypotension is common with antipsychotic use but may occur with multiple classes of medications. The provider could advise the individual to get up from a lying or sitting position slowly. From lying down, suggest they swing their legs over the bed and wait for 30 seconds before standing and then walking.

Sexual side effects. Sexual side effects are common with antidepressants and occasionally with other classes of medications, including antipsychotics. There is a lower than 10% incidence of sexual side effects with buproprion, mirtazapine, and moclobemide. There is a 10–30% incidence with citalopram, escitalopram, duloxetine, and venlafaxine. There is a more than a 30% incidence of sexual side effects with all other SSRIs (Yatham et al., 2009). Onset of sexual side effects is generally not immediate. They also do not tend to improve as treatment continues and can often be dose-dependent.

Identify it as a potential issue for survivors prior to starting the medication. Unless it is addressed early on and in a straightforward manner, survivors are unlikely to identify it as the reason they stop their medications. Provide a space where the survivor feels comfortable broaching the subject later on if needed.

Establish the survivor's baseline level of sexual function for a more accurate review of side effects. Consider lowering the dose of medication if possible and consider switching to a medication with a lower risk of sexual side effects. Consider adding a medication to reduce sexual side effects, such as buproprion, mirtazapine, or buspirone. The prescribing provider may also suggest a trial of one- to two-day "drug holidays" per month to provide a window of opportunity for experiencing lowered sexual side effects.

Suicidal ideation.   One side effect that providers must always monitor closely is the risk of increased suicidal thoughts that occur usually in the first few weeks of therapy on an SSRI. It is best to monitor the survivor closely in the first few weeks of starting any medication and advise them of the possibility of increased suicidal ideation. If they develop increased suicidal ideation, see them immediately and have them stop the medication.

How Quickly Will the Medication Take Effect?

It is not surprising that survivors will ask, "Will these medications start working right away?" It is helpful to give survivors a sense of what to expect with the medication so that they are more aware of the effects and will be prepared for the time that will elapse until it takes effect. For example, anti-depressants may take weeks to improve mood and anxiety, while benzodiazepines will act within hours.

In the context of treating a depressive episode, explain to the survivor that the first one to two weeks of medication initiation is the period of increased likelihood of side effects. Side effects also generally occur when doses are being increased. After the first few weeks, survivors may notice an improvement in sleep and energy level as well as improved appetite. By the third week or so, concentration, interest level, and mood may start to pick up. However, benefits might not be seen for four to six weeks with antidepressants; therefore, aim to keep the survivor's expectations reasonable. Anxiety may take slightly longer to significantly improve with antidepressants, but mild improvement may be seen early on.

It is important to explain the hazards of abruptly discontinuing medication once symptoms have started to improve. Not only might the survivor experience a discontinuation syndrome, but they are also putting themselves at an increased risk of relapse. Any individual who has had one episode of depression is more likely than the average person to have a second episode of depression. The risk of recurrent depression increases with subsequent episodes. In order to address this fact, providers can consider saying something such as the following, "Being on the medication for up to a year, even after you start to feel better, can help protect against a recurrence of your depression in the following five years."

Why Am I Prescribed an Antipsychotic?

A survivor who is prescribed an antipsychotic will naturally ask, "Is that what you think I have?" Medications are often first developed for a specific illness, but over time, as they are studied, the same medication may be used for different purposes. These may be considered "off-label" uses. For example, aspirin was first developed as a pain medication, but over time it became useful to treat other problems. Now, many individuals with heart disease take aspirin daily as a prophylactic, but it is still listed as an "analgesic" or pain medication. The same thing is true with anti-psychotic medications. They were first developed to help treat individuals with psychotic illnesses, such as schizophrenia, but they have been found to be helpful in treating other illnesses and symptoms. They are known to be useful in helping to stabilize mood and anxiety, to manage impulsivity and to assist with sleep.

What if the Medication is Not Right for Me?

Some survivors will say, "This medication just isn't working for me." It is important to explore what the individual's experience has been with the medication and to re-evaluate if this is the right medication for the survivor. Always maintain a welcoming and flexible attitude and respect the survivor's right to choose their own medication regimen. The provider should assist them in weighing the pros and cons of medication treatment, and explore alternate medications or alternate forms of treatment.

Medications can be an important adjunct to therapy for survivors of complex trauma. However, the process of suggesting and choosing medications can trigger trauma memories of being coerced or losing control in the survivor. A thoughtful and flexible approach when discussing or suggesting medications is crucial in helping the survivor explore medication as a part of their treatment plan.

Questions to Think About

1. Some survivors have had the experience of being given non-prescribed psychotropic medications as a part of the abuse they experienced as a child. How might you address this with the survivor and what impact, if any, would it have on your treatment plan?
2. If you prescribe a medication to a survivor and the survivor responds that she does not want to become dependent on the medication, how might you respond?
3. How might you intervene if the survivor reports continued mood swings and feelings of being overwhelmed despite being on medication?
4. In what ways do you apply the principles of trauma-informed care in your role as a prescriber? Are there any changes you can make to your approach to make it more trauma-informed?

11

TRANSFERENCE AND COUNTERTRANSFERENCE

The topic of challenges in the relationship between provider and survivor is generally discussed in the context of mental health services. Consequently, this chapter is written with that context in mind. However, it should be noted that encounters between any individuals in healthcare or social service settings are susceptible to relational challenges, be they doctor/patient or social service worker/client relationships. There are interpersonal dynamics in all relationships. Thus, regardless of setting, all providers can benefit from having a way of understanding the inevitable relational dynamics and feelings that arise between themselves and the individuals with whom they work, but especially when working with survivors of trauma.

Defining Transference and Countertransference

Transference

Transference refers to the phenomenon of the client unconsciously transferring feelings they have about a significant person in their life onto the therapist. These feelings are often based on early relationships and involve unconscious wishes, desires, and fantasies, as well as conscious feelings. The feelings are experienced in the here-and-now, and can feel powerful and even overwhelming. In addition, these feelings usually have some basis in the present relational dynamic (e.g., the female therapist is an authority figure) but will also be strongly influenced by the client's history with an important other (e.g., one's feelings about their mother redirected to the therapist). The client may or may not be aware that the feelings they have towards the therapist are not necessarily entirely about the therapist. This dynamic of the client's transference with the therapist can just as readily be played out by the patient with their physician or the client with their social service provider.

Countertransference

It is important for the provider to recognize that it is not just the client who is susceptible to transferring feelings about an important other onto another person; the provider is also susceptible to the same dynamic of transferring feelings about an important person in their life onto the client. Countertransference is the therapist's (or provider's) transference to the client. Each individual in the dyad—whether it be composed of a client and therapist, patient and physician, or client and social service provider—comes to the therapeutic/healthcare/social service relationship with their own history of relational dynamics, both unconscious and conscious. In all cases, there is the potential for this history to affect the subjective experience of the other in the present relationship. Thus, the survivor can evoke feelings in the provider that are fueled by an important relationship in the provider's life. The provider may find that they have strong feelings directed towards the survivor that are not entirely appropriate to the situation. Similar to the survivor who may or may not be aware that they are experiencing transference, the provider may or may not be aware of how an important outside relationship is influencing their experience of the survivor.

Why it Is Important to Recognize Transference and Countertransference

The dynamics of transference and countertransference are important to recognize because they cannot be avoided. However, they can and should be understood or at least recognized.

Recognizing a transference response from a survivor can be critical to ensuring a good working relationship with the survivor. Recognizing transference enables the provider to step back in order to reflect on the dynamic that is being played out in the relationship. If the provider can understand the nature of the dynamic, then there is the potential for the provider to engage with the survivor in a way that promotes adaptive functioning. The common transferential dynamics for survivors of trauma are discussed below.

It is important for providers to recognize their countertransference so that it does not interfere with the provider/survivor relationship. For example, when the provider recognizes that the strong irritation that they feel is out of proportion to the present circumstances, then the provider can exercise some caution over how they communicate with the survivor. Using a transference/countertransference framework for self-reflection, the provider might ask themselves, "Who is the survivor reminding me of from my personal history?" Often, it is enough just to recognize that the feelings are too strong to be simply about the present relationship. Recognizing the dynamics can assist the provider to respond to the survivor in the most appropriate and helpful way.

Understanding the Provider/Survivor Relationship Using a Trauma Framework

Working with survivors of trauma can evoke unique relational dynamics. An important dynamic to recognize is when the survivor "reenacts" some aspect of the interpersonal trauma. A reenactment is the "unconscious recreation in the treatment setting of dissociatedly unavailable aspects of self and object representations [which] . . . volley back and forth between client and therapist in startling reconstructions of early trauma . . ." (Davies & Frawley, 1994, p.3). A reenactment is when both the survivor and provider get caught in a traumatic transference; the survivor experiences the provider in a way that is similar to a traumatic aspect of a historical relationship, and the provider finds themselves pulled into a dynamic with the survivor that may feel out of proportion to the situation.

Karpman's Triangle

Karpman's triangle (Karpman, 1968) is a useful model for conceptualizing reenactments in the therapeutic relationship with survivors. This model (Figure 11.1; Appendix G) characterizes the roles of different relational dynamics often experienced with trauma survivors. Victim, persecutor, and rescuer are the roles identified by Karpman, and any combination of two of these can be experienced in the therapeutic dyad. Davies and Frawley (1994) identified and added a fourth position, the uninvolved/neglectful bystander, to these three positions. This is a role which many survivors recognize, representing, for example, the neglectful parent who turned a blind eye to the abuse.

The relational dynamics captured by Karpman's triangle are inevitable when working with survivors. Over the course of therapy, these reenactments are not

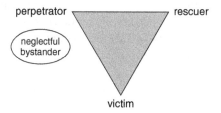

FIGURE 11.1 Modified Karpman's triangle to illustrate common traumatic reenactments. Stephen B. Karpman, M.D. uses the terms victim, persecutor, and rescuer. We have changed persecutor to perpetrator. While the term persecutor reflects harassing or oppressive behaviour (which can certainly be abusive), the term perpetrator more fully encompasses the severity of chronic abuse and better reflects the dynamics experienced by trauma survivors. In addition, we have added the position of the neglectful bystander to Karpman's Drama Triangle.

Source: Karpman Drama Triangle. Copyright © 1967–2008, 2011 by Stephen B. Karpman, M.D.

something to be ignored or avoided; rather their emergence and processing are an intrinsic part of the treatment (Chu, 1998). However, in short-term therapy or other non-mental health clinical encounters, there is usually not enough time to adequately process these dynamics. Nonetheless, it is helpful to have an understanding of this framework while working with survivors.

This is a useful framework for exploring reenactments with the provider or relational difficulties in the survivor's outside life. Any of these roles can be cast onto the provider or survivor and roles can switch quickly. In fact, one can easily go from being the victim to the perpetrator when the person becomes frustrated or angry in response to feeling victimized. This framework can be helpful in the provider's self-reflection. For example, those who aim to hold a neutral stance may inadvertently feed into a dynamic in which they are seen as a neglectful or uncaring bystander.

Awareness of the survivor's transference and the provider's countertransference is valuable when in a reenactment. How the survivor experiences the provider can give important information about how the survivor feels about themselves in this dynamic. Equally important is how the provider feels. For example, if the provider feels the urge to save or rescue the survivor, or feels powerless or ineffective, this is important information for the relationship. With greater awareness about when and how the survivor and provider get caught in these dynamics, the survivor can begin the hard work of disengaging from these dynamics. Moreover, information regarding the dynamic between the provider and survivor can be essential in letting the provider know if they are stuck in Karpman's triangle. By exploring these dynamics with the survivor, the survivor can better understand these relational patterns and how they might be getting in the way of having healthy relationships.

A Description of Four Potential Roles in Traumatic Reenactments

For each of the four roles (victim, perpetrator, rescuer, neglectful bystander), a list of descriptions capturing the range of emotional states that are possible when in that role are provided below. In addition, examples are provided of how these dynamics might play out in one's work with a survivor (Davies & Frawley, 1994).

Victim role. A person caught in the victim role may feel any of the following:

- Powerless;
- Oppressed;
- Helpless;
- Hopeless;
- Victimized;
- Vulnerable;
- Scared or fearful;
- Weak;
- Devalued;

- Disrespected;
- Used;
- Self-blaming;
- Trapped;
- Paralyzed;
- Ineffective;
- Despairing;
- Deflated;
- Own feelings are less important than the other's feelings.

Following are examples of how the provider might feel if caught in the victim role with the survivor:

- The provider feels unwanted, unhelpful, or unimportant to the survivor;
- The provider finds themselves working extremely hard to make a connection with the survivor;
- The provider feels like giving up, or as if there is no use.

Following are examples of how the survivor might feel when in the victim role in the relationship with the provider:

- The survivor denies their feelings, putting the needs of the provider first;
- The survivor feels as though they must be "good" in order to maintain the relationship; the survivor may then act out after the session (e.g., with self-harm);
- The survivor experiences the provider as intentionally hurting them, or feels as though they are not heard or seen. This can often occur if there is an empathic disconnection or the provider is unable to respond in the way the survivor hopes;
- Survivors may also enter the session expecting their needs to be unmet, as this is a familiar pattern. Subsequently, they may only notice the interactions that fit this pattern and not the other aspects of the experience which might challenge this pattern.

Perpetrator role. A person caught in the perpetrator role may feel or experience any of the following:

- All-powerful;
- Controlling;
- Invasive;
- Intruding;
- Crosses boundaries;
- Demanding;
- Manipulative;
- Abusive;

- Angry;
- Destructive;
- Harming.

Following are examples of how a provider might feel or behave if they are in the perpetrator role:

- An overactive and intrusive provider who is steadfast about not being similar to the survivor's neglectful parent, and instead ends up controlling the session and the survivor;
- A provider who hospitalizes the survivor for self-harming. (Note that feeling like a perpetrator may occur even while the provider knows that they are doing the right thing;
- A provider who erupts after weeks of being dismissed or insulted by the survivor. Here, the provider has changed roles from being the victim to becoming the abuser, and the abusive survivor becomes the victim.

Following are examples of how the survivor might feel or behave if they are in the role of a perpetrator:

- The survivor intrudes on a provider's personal or professional life;
- The survivor engages in entitled demands for the provider's time;
- The survivor threatens termination or other forms of retaliation (e.g., litigation) for a felt injury.

Rescuer role.   A person caught in the rescuer role may feel like any of the following:

- A caretaker;
- A saviour;
- An omnipotent protector;
- They are essentially needed by the other;
- They have a special role or connection with the other;
- They are guilty of making the other feel difficult feelings, suggesting they have inordinate power over the other.

Following are examples of how a provider may feel or behave if in the role of a rescuer:

- The provider has the wish (even fleeting) to bring a survivor home with him/her;
- The provider has the urge to protect the survivor from certain feelings;
- The provider gives extra time to an upset survivor. While it is important be responsive to a survivor's distress, such as when helping the survivor find a way to calm down and ground themselves, a provider who frequently

has difficulty managing time during the meeting and routinely overextends their time with an upset survivor can be responding as a rescuer. Instead of empowering the survivor to self-soothe, the provider's inadvertent message may be that the survivor is too damaged to take care of themselves and that they need rescuing.

Following are examples of how the survivor may feel or behave when in the role of a rescuer:

- The survivor is overly attuned to and sensitive towards the provider's mood and needs;
- The survivor responds in a caring and loving way to any perceived stress in the provider's life, as though it is the client's responsibility to make the provider feel better;
- The survivor protects the provider from the horrific details of their trauma history.

Neglectful bystander role. A person caught in the neglectful bystander role may experience any of the following:

- Feels dismissive of the other;
- "Misses" the other (i.e., does not recognize what is going on with the other);
- Does not see or hear the other;
- Is forgetful;
- Has an inadequate response or displays inadequate caring;
- Does not address the other's needs;
- Feels bored, annoyed, or is angered by the other's needs;
- Is withholding;
- Expects others to cope on their own.

Following are examples of what the provider might experience when in the role of a neglectful bystander:

- The provider feels uninterested or bored by the survivor;
- The provider forgets important details of the survivor's life;
- The provider is unusually tired in session or watching the clock.

Following are examples of what the survivor might experience when in the role of a neglectful bystander:

- The survivor is bored or irritated with the therapist's interest or questions;
- The survivor dismisses their own vulnerabilities as unimportant.

Karpman's triangle represents some of the common difficulties a provider may face when working with survivors of trauma. Survivors often have rigid understandings of relationships, and providers might inadvertently feed this misunderstanding. For example, trauma survivors might implicitly (or explicitly) believe that there is always one person who holds the power and another who is powerless, or that there needs to be someone who can rescue them. This framework can be explored with the survivor. Below we discuss how to break free from Karpman's triangle.

Breaking Free from Traumatic Reenactments

Ideally, in traumatic reenactments, the provider will intervene in order to get the relationship unstuck. Once free from the reenactment, the pattern can be explored if it is appropriate to the situation and if time permits.

For each reenactment position, there is a different prescription for how both providers and survivors can get out of the reenactment (Davies & Frawley, 1994). (Figure 11.2; Appendix H) It should be noted that working through a reenactment takes a certain amount of time and trust in the relationship, neither of which may be possible when working in some healthcare settings. For example, in urgent care there is sometimes only one encounter with the survivor. Nevertheless, even though the situation might not provide sufficient time or trust, it may be possible to apply the strategies described below if only at a cursory level.

Perpetrators should empathize. Abusers disregard their victims' feelings and the impact of their actions on the other. In order to get out of the perpetrator position in Karpman's triangle, the provider should empathize with the survivor. If the provider does not identify with the role of perpetrator (i.e. cannot recognize any feelings within themselves that align with the perpetrator role) but the survivor is acting as if the provider is a perpetrator, it is important for the provider to pause and imagine some of the possible feelings that the survivor could be having in

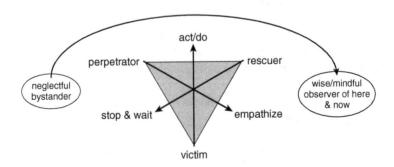

FIGURE 11.2 Strategies for getting out of a traumatic reenactment.

response to the provider. By putting themselves in the place of the survivor, the provider may be able to identify what it is about the provider (or the situation) that could lead to the survivor feeling victimized. Conveying an understanding to the survivor of how the survivor is likely feeling, and of how the provider might be contributing to the survivor's sense of being a victim, is essential for extricating oneself from the perpetrator role and setting the stage for the survivor to step out of the victim role. To summarize:

- The provider should work on developing feelings of empathy toward the survivor;
- The provider should understand and validate the feelings of the survivor;
- The provider should imagine what it would feel like to have the survivor's perception of the situation or to experience the provider in this way;
- The provider should put aside defensiveness and not argue about the accuracy of perception.

Victims should act/do. Victims have been stripped of their power and are defenseless against what was done to them. If the provider is in the role of the victim, they should work to find some degree of freedom, choice, and action. For example, finding one's voice, even if to articulate how one is feeling, is an example of acting or doing. The provider might find a way to resist or defend themselves by, for example, setting limits on overtly abusive behaviour. Silence can also be a powerful defense or resistance if deliberately and freely chosen. Although it may be uncomfortable for the provider to feel like a victim, there is often something important to be learned from this experience. It gives the provider an opportunity to understand how the survivor often feels. To summarize:

- Feeling victimized is central to the survivor's traumatic history and it is helpful for the provider to have a visceral understanding of it;
- The provider should set limits on the things the survivor does or says that are overtly abusive;
- The provider should share their experience of feeling like a victim to help the survivor understand the dynamic. This will help foster empathy, which is the way out of the perpetrator role.

If the survivor is in the victim role, the provider should help the survivor identify any action they could take to regain power. Alternatively, the provider might help the survivor reframe their behaviour in an empowering way, such as framing silence as a powerful form of defense or resistance.

Rescuers should stop and wait. Often, rescuers feel powerful and compelled to intervene in order to "save the day," which disempowers the victim. They may feel an urge to protect the survivor from their feelings or to give them special treatment. In order to get out of Karpman's triangle, the provider should stop and re-engage with the survivor in a collaborative fashion that encourages their empowerment and choice. The provider should notice any urges and impulses and then wait. The dynamic that the provider is in with the survivor may be a reflection of the provider's psychology, the survivor's psychology or both. For instance, is the survivor wishing to be rescued? Alternatively, the urge to rescue might be a reflection of the provider's own history (i.e., countertransference). For example, is it a reflection of the provider's discomfort with feeling helpless in the face of another's suffering? The rescuer role might be a role that healthcare and social service providers are especially vulnerable to given their chosen profession. To summarize:

- The provider should acknowledge to themselves the urge to protect the survivor or to give them special treatment;
- The provider should support the survivor to feel empowered to face their own struggles and to heal;
- The provider should ask themselves whether this dynamic is reminiscent of other dynamics for the survivor or for the provider;
- The provider should explore what the survivor can do in order to rescue themselves.

Neglectful bystander should become the mindful or wise observer. The neglectful bystander is often disengaged and indifferent and remains caught in a state of inaction. In order to get out of the reenactment the neglectful bystander needs to notice what is happening. Once they notice and become aware of the re-enactment dynamic, they can become the wise observer and make a conscious decision to engage with the survivor in the here-and-now. The provider should notice their own feelings and thoughts, such as feelings of detachment or boredom or that they are distracted and their mind is elsewhere. It is also important for the provider to recognize and acknowledge the survivor. Is there something about the survivor that is making it difficult for the provider to remain engaged? What might the survivor be attempting to communicate with their behaviour? The provider should be curious with themselves and with the survivor about what is going on between them. This will provide an opportunity to identify the dynamic and to make a different choice about how to engage. To summarize:

- The provider should acknowledge their thoughts and feelings;
- The provider should ask the survivor about their experience in that moment;
- The provider should recognize and acknowledge the survivor;
- The provider should engage the survivor in being curious and exploring the relational dynamic that they are caught in;
- The provider should identify the dynamic and, together with the survivor, make conscious choices based in the here-and-now.

Relational dynamics are inevitable between individuals. This chapter has outlined some of the common dynamics that can arise when working with survivors of trauma. Having an understanding of these dynamics can help the provider recognize when they may be engaged in a traumatic reenactment. With this recognition, the provider and survivor then have the opportunity to step out of the enactment and engage in a healthier way in the here-and-now. In the next chapter we will look at the impact of vicarious traumatization.

Questions to Think About

1. Reflect on why transference and countertransference are important issues to be aware of when treating traumatized individuals?
2. What supports do you have or can you develop that would permit you to discuss transference and countertransference issues in your work with survivors?
3. Identify some indicators in your working relationship with a survivor that would suggest to you that you may be caught in a reenactment of past trauma with the survivor.
4. Reflect on the countertransference signals in your thoughts and feelings that might indicate that you and the survivor may be caught in a reenactment of past trauma.

12

UNDERSTANDING VICARIOUS TRAUMATIZATION

The motivation for working in any of the helping professions is often the desire to help others. However, responding to the urgent needs of others, hearing about traumatic experiences, and wanting to help and sometimes not knowing how to do so can be taxing on the provider. Through exposure to traumatic stories and their effects, the provider's empathic connection with the survivor can cause the provider to experience feelings of loss, betrayal and hurt. Empathy is how providers connect to those with whom they work, but it is also what makes them vulnerable to vicarious traumatization.

Saakvitne and her colleagues define vicarious traumatization as "the transformation or change in a helper's inner experience as a result of responsibility for and empathic engagement with traumatized clients" (Saakvitne, Gamble, Pearlman, & Lev, 2000, p. 157). They believe it is an inescapable effect of working with survivors, and an inevitable hazard of doing trauma therapy. Vicarious traumatization is not something that is done to the provider by the survivor. Rather, it is a consequence of the provider's caring, being connected to and opening their own eyes to the experience of trauma (Saakvitne & Pearlman, 1996). It is also a process and not an event (Saakvitne et al., 2000).

Vicarious traumatization can be difficult for providers to talk about. Some may avoid telling colleagues for fear of being seen as a failed provider who is "not cut out for this type of work," weak, or too sensitive. This can leave providers feeling alone with their feelings of vicarious traumatization, and may reinforce a sense that it is something bad that needs to be hidden. In fact it is an inevitable hazard of working with trauma survivors. False beliefs about vicarious traumatization may have been inadvertently developed during the provider's professional training if, as learners, they were told that they "should leave the work at the office" or simply move on to the next client and put it behind them. What was likely intended as a helpful suggestion offered to those in training is actually unhelpful and detrimental to the provider's mental health and ability to competently perform their job.

Why Is it Important to Address Vicarious Traumatization?

Vicarious traumatization is important to address because it affects the provider's personal and professional life. The symptoms experienced by healthcare providers, mental health providers and social service providers are similar to those experienced by individuals who have experienced trauma directly. These symptoms affect the provider's daily life, including their beliefs about and experiences of the self, others, and the world. Professionally, unaddressed vicarious trauma can be a significant contributor to "burnout" (Neumann & Gamble, 1995). Providers have an ethical obligation to address their vicarious traumatization. They have a duty to themselves, to the survivors they work with, and to those in their personal lives to not become damaged by this work (Saakvitne et al., 2000).

If vicarious traumatization is not addressed, providers are more likely to become overwhelmed by their work. Without realizing it, the provider can develop the tendency to self-protect against painful feelings by shutting down or acting out. When overwhelmed, they are more likely to fall back on an "us versus them" thinking about those with whom they work. When providers distance themselves from survivors by treating them as "other," this attempt at self-protection necessarily erodes the provider's capacity for empathy. In addition, vicarious traumatization can cause providers to be less self-reflective and rely more on rigid rules as a means of gaining a sense of control. These tendencies can lead to disempowerment of and disconnection from the survivor, and run counter to the principles of trauma-informed care, the goal of which is to foster empowerment, choice, and connection.

Indicators of Vicarious Traumatization

The same areas of functioning that are affected in trauma survivors are also affected in providers with vicarious traumatization. Thus, vicarious traumatization can affect the provider's frame of reference, self-capacities, ego resources, psychological needs, cognitive schemas, perception, and memory (Saakvitne & Pearlman, 1996). It can be different for each individual. The following list is compiled from two sources: a workbook for vicarious traumatization and *Risking connection: A training curriculum for working with survivors of childhood abuse* (Saakvitne & Pearlman, 1996). This list outlines the myriad ways in which vicarious traumatization can manifest for providers (Saakvitne & Pearlman, 1996; Saakvitne et al., 2000, pages 168–169) including:

- Intrusive experiences, such as dreams about survivors with whom they work, nightmares, or recounting the details of survivors' traumas;

- Strong reactions and feelings, such as grief, anger, shock, or sadness;
- Emotional numbing, feeling "shut down";
- Loss of hope;
- Feelings of despair and hopelessness;
- Feeling guilty for the privileges they have (e.g., safe home growing up, supportive relationships);
- Loss of meaning;
- Being easily overwhelmed by feelings;
- Sensitivity to and avoidance of violence (e.g., news, movies, stories);
- Change in the provider's core beliefs about safety, trust, esteem, intimacy, and control (e.g., nowhere is safe; no one can be trusted; all people are cruel; I must control everything or I'll be controlled);
- Avoidance of intimacy;
- Feeling as though they have no time or energy for themselves;
- Withdrawing from others;
- Cynicism or pessimism;
- Loss of a sense of spirituality;
- Reduced sense of respect for the people with whom they work;
- Loss of enjoyment of sexual activity;
- Feeling they cannot discuss work with family or friends;
- Finding they talk about work too much;
- Increased sense of danger (reduced sense of safety);
- Increased fear for safety of children or loved ones;
- Increased illness or fatigue, aches, and pains;
- Increased absenteeism (sick days);
- Greater problems with boundaries and limit-setting (either at work or at home);
- Difficulty making decisions, or making poor decisions;
- Reduced productivity;
- Reduced motivation for work;
- Loss of control over work and life in general;
- Lowered self-esteem, lowered sense of competence in one's work;
- Difficulty trusting others;
- Reduced interest in spending time alone;
- Less time spent reflecting on their own experiences.

Self-Assessment of Vicarious Traumatization

It is important for providers to assess their own vicarious traumatization. The list above can be used as a way to self-assess vicarious traumatization. Providers are advised to read through the list and make note of those signs and symptoms they may be experiencing as a result of their work. The items that providers identify as relevant to themselves may indicate the areas that the provider should address in order to take care of themselves. It can be helpful to share responses with trusted colleagues, especially if the provider has endorsed many of the indicators, or to review this list every month with each other.

Providers and their colleagues should be encouraged to have discussions about vicarious traumatization. If this issue is understood and recognized to be a predictable and normal part of the work that they do, then this opens the door to coming up with ways to address it. This includes creating mechanisms for mutual support with colleagues and even to explore avenues to gain systemic support in the place of work.

Other assessment tools have been created to assess vicarious traumatization. The Professional Quality of Life Scale (ProQOL 5) is a commonly used measure of the negative and positive effects of working with survivors of trauma. This assessment explores three concepts that are related to vicarious traumatization: compassion fatigue, burnout, and compassion satisfaction. Compassion fatigue is similar to vicarious traumatization, addressing the traumatization of the helping professional. Burnout refers to emotional exhaustion and reduced work-related motivation, esteem, and accomplishment. Compassion satisfaction is the positive sense of fulfillment from one's work. This assessment is available for free online at: http://www.proqol.org/ProQol_Test.html.

Strategies for Addressing Vicarious Traumatization

There are two strategies for addressing vicarious traumatization:

1. Practice self-care in order to mitigate the inherent stress of trauma work; and
2. Address the loss of hope and demoralization that result from doing trauma-focused work.

Both components are essential and build upon each other. Practicing self-care can increase hope and bring a sense of meaning to one's life, and addressing feelings of hopelessness, meaninglessness, and demoralization can be nurturing and self-soothing (Saakvitne & Pearlman, 1996).

Practice Self-Care

Self-care will improve one's quality of life and decrease stress. Self-care includes setting limits or boundaries around trauma work in order to accomplish the following: achieve a balance between work and one's life outside of work; engage in healthy habits; and ensure that connection with others is maintained. It can also include nurturing activities such as doing things that are pleasurable and that encourage relaxation and comfort. Finally, self-care can include escape, which allows one to get away from work and from associated painful feelings by indulging in fantasy and play (Saakvitne & Pearlman, 1996).

Address Loss of Hope and Demoralization

The loss of hope and demoralization that occur with vicarious traumatization can be experienced as nihilism, cynicism, and despair (Saakvitne & Pearlman, 1996). Engaging in activities that are infused with meaning, or creating meaningful activities, can combat these feelings. Engaging in creative activities can provide an antidote to despair. Working with trauma survivors can be difficult work, but it is also rewarding. A provider can be deeply adversely affected by this work, as we have seen in the discussion of the indicators of vicarious traumatization in providers. The opposite, however, is also true. Engaging in therapeutic work opens providers up to the power of connection, the incredible resilience of human beings, and to hope and healing.

As a responsible provider, it is important to address vicarious traumatization and challenge any barriers to addressing it. Just as survivors are encouraged to engage in open discussion of trauma and traumatization, providers need to be open and supportive of one another regarding vicarious traumatization in order to normalize this common experience. Providers are encouraged to explore vicarious traumatization with their colleagues, educate others on this issue, and work together to find ways to address vicarious traumatization in the workplace.

Addressing Vicarious Traumatization at the Organizational Level

An organization can either support the needs of employees or exacerbate vicarious traumatization. Addressing vicarious traumatization must occur at the individual and organizational level. An organization can demonstrate support through both attitudinal and practical interventions. Bloom and Farragher (2013) advocate applying the principles of trauma-informed care to support and enhance resilience on an organizational level. Below are some suggestions for addressing and preventing vicarious traumatization (Saakvitne et al., 2000, p. 184):

- Provide adequate clinical supervision for all staff;
- Create a climate that accepts that this work will elicit strong feelings and provides a safe setting in which to discuss such feelings;
- Offer health benefits that include adequate coverage for mental health services;
- Explicitly acknowledge the difficulty of the work;
- Use staffing patterns that allow backup and sharing of clinical responsibilities and coverage;
- Set reasonable expectations for clinical caseloads (i.e., expectations that take into account the potential for vicarious traumatization);
- Affirm the reality, pervasiveness, and severity of the effects of interpersonal trauma;
- Work with staff to identify and address signs of vicarious traumatization; and

- Provide opportunities for continuing education in the area of trauma and of stress management.

Vicarious traumatization is an inevitable part of working in the helping profession. When providers take care of themselves, build meaning in their work and personal lives, and support their colleagues to have open dialogue about the reality of this work, this can allow the provider to fully experience the powerful encounters with survivors at work, individuals in their personal life, and themselves.

Questions to Think About

1. Reflect on your professional training and what messages, if any, you received about the provider's self-care. Did you learn about the potential for vicarious traumatization?
2. Reflect on how your work with traumatized clients has affected your beliefs and behaviours.
3. Is there support in your workplace for discussing the effects of vicarious trauma and support for finding a balance in your work and life outside of work? If not, how can you start to develop these supports?
4. What steps can you take to deal with vicarious trauma and to learn to care for yourself?

APPENDIX A

Posttraumatic Stress Disorder
Diagnostic Criteria

Posttraumatic Stress Disorder

Diagnostic Criteria 309.81 (F43.10)

Note: The following criteria apply to adults, adolescents, and children older than six years. (For children six years or younger, see corresponding criteria.)

A. Exposure to actual or threatened death, serious injury, or sexual violation in one (or more) of the following ways:
   1. Directly experiencing the traumatic event(s).
   2. Witnessing, in person, the event(s) as it occurred to others.
   3. Learning that the event(s) occurred to a close family member or close friend.
       Note: In cases of actual or threatened death of a family member or friend, the event(s) must have been violent or accidental.
   4. Experiencing repeated or extreme exposure to aversive details of the traumatic event(s) (e.g., first responders collecting human remains, police officers repeatedly exposed to details of child abuse).
       Note: Criterion A4 does not apply to exposure through electronic media, television, movies or pictures, unless this exposure is work related.

B. Presence of one (or more) of the following intrusion symptoms associated with traumatic events), beginning after the traumatic event(s) occurred:
   1. Recurrent, involuntary, and intrusive distressing memories of the traumatic event(s).
       Note: In children, repetitive play may occur in which themes or aspects of the traumatic event(s) are expressed.
   2. Recurrent distressing dreams in which the content and/or affect of the dream are related to the event(s).
       Note: in children, there may be frightening dreams without recognizable content.

    3. Dissociative reactions (e.g., flashbacks) in which the individual feels or acts as if the traumatic event(s) were recurring. (Such reactions may occur on a continuum, with the most extreme expression being a complete loss of awareness of present surroundings.)
Note: In children, trauma-specific reenactments may occur in play.

    4. Intense or prolonged psychological distress or marked physiological reactions in response to internal or external cues that symbolize or resemble an aspect of the traumatic event(s).

    5. Marked physiological reactions to internal or external cues that symbolize or resemble an aspect of the traumatic event(s).

C. Persistent avoidance of stimuli associated with the traumatic events(s), beginning after the traumatic event(s) occurred, as evidenced by one or both of the following:

    6. Avoidance of or efforts to avoid distressing memories, thoughts, or feelings about or closely associated with the traumatic event(s).

    7. Avoidance of or efforts to avoid external reminders (e.g., people, places, conversations activities, objects, situations) that arouse distressing memories, thoughts or feelings about or closely associated with the traumatic event(s).

D. Negative alterations in cognitions and mood associated with the traumatic event(s), beginning or worsening after the traumatic event(s) occurred, as evidenced by two (or more) of the following:

    1. Inability to remember an important aspect of the traumatic event(s) (typically due to dissociative amnesia and not to other factors such as head injury, alcohol, or drugs).

    2. Persistent and exaggerated negative beliefs or expectations about oneself, others, or the world (e.g., "I am bad," "No one can be trusted," "The world is completely dangerous," "My whole nervous system is permanently ruined").

    3. Persistent, distorted cognitions about the cause or consequences of the traumatic event(s) that lead the individual to blame himself/herself or others.

    4. Persistent negative emotional state (e.g., fear, horror, anger, guilt, or shame).

    5. Markedly diminished interest or participation in significant activities.

    6. Feelings of detachment or estrangement from others.

    7. Persistent inability to experience positive emotions (e.g., inability to experience happiness, satisfaction, or loving feelings).

E. Marked alterations in arousal and reactivity associated with the traumatic event(s) beginning or worsening after the traumatic event(s) occurred, as evidenced by two (or more) of the following:

    1. Irritable behaviour and angry outbursts (with little or no provocation), typically expressed as verbal or physical aggression toward people or objects.

    2. Reckless or self-destructive behaviour.

    3. Hypervigilance.

    4. Exaggerated startle response.

    5. Problems with concentration.

    6. Sleep disturbance (e.g., difficulty falling or staying sleep, restless sleep).

F. Duration of the disturbance (Criterion B, C, D, and E) is more than one month.

G. The disturbance causes clinically significant distress or impairment in the social, occupational or other important areas of functioning.

H. The disturbance is not attributable to the physiological effect of a substance (e.g., medication, alcohol) or another medical condition.

Specify whether:

With dissociative symptoms: The individual's symptoms meet the criteria for posttraumatic stress disorder, and in addition, in response to the stressor, the individual experiences persistent or recurrent symptoms of either of the following:

1. **Depersonalization:** Persistent or recurrent experiences of feeling detached from, and as if one were an outside observer of, one's mental processes or body (e.g., feeling as though one were in a dream; feeling a sense of unreality of self or body or of time moving slowly).
2. **Derealization:** Persistent or recurrent experiences of unreality of surroundings (e.g., the world around the individual is experienced as unreal, dreamlike, distant or distorted).

Note: to use this subtype, the dissociative symptoms must not be attributable to the physiological effect of a substance (e.g., blackouts, behaviour during alcohol intoxication) or another medical condition (e.g., complex partial seizures).

Specify if:

With delayed expression: If the full diagnostic criteria are not met until at least six months after the event (although the onset and expression of some symptoms may be immediate).

(DSM–5, American Psychiatric Association, 2013)

APPENDIX B

Acute Stress Disorder Diagnostic Criteria

Acute Stress Disorder

Diagnostic Criteria 308.3 (F43.0)

A. Exposure to actual or threatened death, serious injury, or sexual violation in one (or more) of the following ways:
    1. Directly experiencing the traumatic event(s).
    2. Witnessing, in person, the event(s) as it occurred to others.
    3. Learning that the event(s) occurred to a close family member or close friend.
        Note: In cases of actual or threatened death of a family member or friend, the event(s) must have been violent or accidental.
    4. Experiencing repeated or extreme exposure to aversive details of the traumatic event(s) (e.g., first responders collecting human remains, police officers repeatedly exposed to details of child abuse).
        Note: This does not apply to exposure through electronic media, television, movies or pictures, unless this exposure is work related.

B. Presence of nine (or more) of the following symptoms from any of the five categories of intrusion, negative mood, dissociation, avoidance, and arousal, beginning or worsening after the traumatic event(s) occurred:

Intrusion Symptoms

1. Recurrent, involuntary, and intrusive distressing memories of the traumatic event(s).
    Note: In children, repetitive play may occur in which themes or aspects of the traumatic event(s) are expressed.
2. Recurrent distressing dreams in which the content and/or effect of the dream are related to the event(s).
    Note: In children, there may be frightening dreams without recognizable content.

3. Dissociative reactions (e.g., flashbacks) in which the individual feels or acts as if the traumatic event(s) were recurring. (Such reactions may occur on a continuum, with the most extreme expression being a complete loss of awareness of present surroundings.)
   Note: In children, trauma-specific reenactments may occur in play.
4. Intense or prolonged psychological distress or marked physiological reactions in response to internal or external cues that symbolize or resemble an aspect of the traumatic event(s).

Negative Mood

5. Persistent inability to experience positive emotions (e.g., inability to experience happiness, satisfaction, or loving feelings).

Dissociative Symptoms

6. An altered sense of the reality of one's surroundings of oneself (e.g., seeing oneself from another perspective, being in a daze, time slowing).
7. Inability to remember an important aspect of the traumatic event(s) (typically due to dissociative amnesia and not to other factors such as head injury, alcohol, or drugs).

Avoidance Symptoms

8. Efforts to avoid distressing memories, thoughts, or feelings about or closely associated with the traumatic event(s).
9. Efforts to avoid external reminders (e.g., people, places, conversations activities, objects, situations) that arouse distressing memories, thoughts or feelings about or closely associated with the traumatic event(s).

Arousal Symptoms

10. Sleep disturbance (e.g., difficulty falling or staying sleep, restless sleep).
11. Irritable behaviour and angry outbursts (with little or no provocation), typically expressed as verbal or physical aggression toward people or objects.
12. Hypervigilance.
13. Problems with concentration.
14. Exaggerated startle response.

C. Duration of the disturbance (Symptoms in Criterion B) is three days to one month after trauma exposure.
   Note: Symptoms typically begin immediately after the trauma, but persistence for at least three days and up to a month is needed to meet disorder criteria.
D. The disturbance causes clinically significant distress or impairment in social, occupational, or other important areas of functioning.
E. The disturbance is not attributable to the physiological effects of a substance (e.g., medication or alcohol) or another medical condition (e.g., mild traumatic brain injury) and is not better explained by brief psychotic disorder.

(DSM-5, American Psychiatric Association, 2013)

APPENDIX C

Dissociative Identity Disorder Diagnostic Criteria

Dissociative Identity Disorder

Diagnostic Criteria 300.14 (F44.81)

A. Disruption of identity characterized by two or more distinct personality states, which may be described in some cultures as an experience of possession. The disruption in identity involves marked discontinuity in sense of self and sense of agency, accompanied by related alterations in affect, behaviour, consciousness, memory, perception, cognition, and/or sensory-motor functioning. These signs and symptoms may be observed by others or reported by the individual.

B. Recurrent gaps in the recall of everyday events, important personal information, and/or traumatic events that are inconsistent with ordinary forgetting.

C. The symptoms cause clinically significant distress or impairment in social, occupational, or other important areas of functioning.

D. The disturbance is not a normal part of a broadly accepted cultural or religious practice.
    Note: In children, the symptoms are not better explained by imaginary playmates or other fantasy play.

E. The symptoms are not attributable to the physiological effects of a substance (e.g., blackouts or chaotic behaviour during alcohol intoxication) or another medical condition (e.g., complex partial seizures).

(DSM-5, American Psychiatric Association, 2013).

APPENDIX D

Trauma and the Hijacked Brain: The High Road and the Low Road

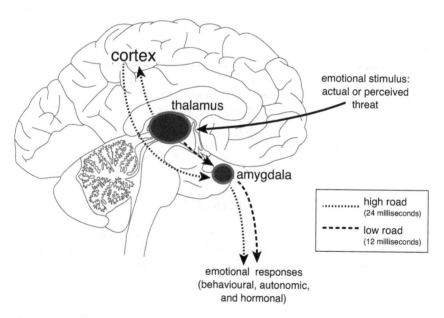

When triggered by fearful stimuli there are two paths of information processing—the low road is an instinctive survival response and the high road involves cortical assessment (LeDoux, 1996).

APPENDIX E

Window of Tolerance

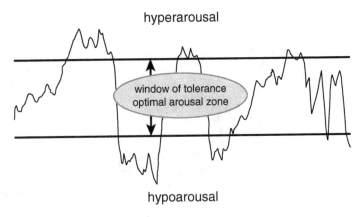

hyperarousal

window of tolerance
optimal arousal zone

hypoarousal

This model depicts three zones of arousal: hyperarousal, hypoarousal, and the optimal arousal. This model is useful when explaining symptoms of PTSD and the common experience of trauma survivors' dysregulated arousal (Ogden, Minton, & Pain, 2006).

APPENDIX F

Trigger Scale

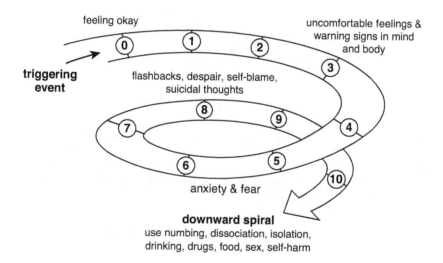

feeling okay

uncomfortable feelings & warning signs in mind and body

triggering event

flashbacks, despair, self-blame, suicidal thoughts

anxiety & fear

downward spiral
use numbing, dissociation, isolation, drinking, drugs, food, sex, self-harm

Survivors of trauma can identify their subjective experience at each stage on the trigger (e.g., individual signs and symptoms of distress).

APPENDIX G

Modified Karpman's Triangle to Illustrate Common Traumatic Reenactments

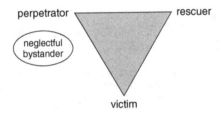

Stephen B. Karpman, M.D., uses the terms victim, persecutor, and rescuer. We have changed persecutor to perpetrator. While the term persecutor reflects harassing or oppressive behaviour (which can certainly be abusive), the term perpetrator more fully encompasses the severity of chronic abuse and better reflects the dynamics experienced by trauma survivors. In addition, we have added the position of the neglectful bystander to Karpman's Drama Triangle.

Source: Karpman Drama Triangle. Copyright © 1967–2008, 2011 by Stephen B. Karpman, M.D.

APPENDIX H

Strategies for Getting Out of a Traumatic Reenactment

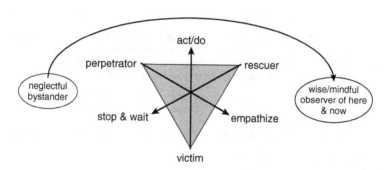

This figure describes how to get out of Karpman's triangle. Each position requires an opposite action in order to step out of the reenactment.

APPENDIX I

Self-soothing Strategies

Here is a list of different strategies you can use to self-soothe. When you are upset it might be hard to think about what would make you feel better. Try a number of these and learn which ones work best for you. If one of these isn't helpful, try another one. Feel free to add self-soothing strategies that you find are helpful.

1. Mindful breathing—Follow your breath. Inhale through your nose, then slowly exhale through your mouth. Count to three for your inhale, and count to five for your exhale.
2. Talk to someone supportive (a friend, family member, counsellor, 24-hour crisis line, support group member).
3. Have a hot shower or bath.
4. Have a cup of herbal tea or warm soothing beverage.
5. Stroke the cat or pet the dog.
6. Listen to relaxing music.
7. Read affirmations or write your favourite affirmations out 100 times (i.e., I am safe. It's safe for me to relax now. I am not to I blame . . .).
8. Go for a walk, a bike ride, or a jog.
9. Punch or yell into a pillow.
10. Pound on your bed, throw ice cubes into the bathtub.
11. Pray or meditate.
12. Go to a place where you feel comfortable and safe (i.e., your favourite room, rocking chair, bed, your friend's house).
13. Watch an old movie or read a novel.
14. Write in your journal.
15. Pamper yourself.
16. Go to the gym, do aerobics or some activity that raises your heart rate.

APPENDIX J

Relaxation Strategies

The next time you notice the beginning signs of distress, try one or more of these relaxation strategies.

Deep Breathing

Follow these simple steps:
1. Sit or stand comfortably.
2. Inhale slowly through the nose (and push out stomach).
3. Hold for a few seconds.
4. Exhale through pursed lips slowly.
5. Repeat several times.
6. Shift concentration from breathing to feelings of relaxation in your body.

Progressive Relaxation

Follow these simple steps:
1. Inhale and tense muscles of brow and around eyes and notice how it feels.
2. Hold tension for five seconds.
3. Exhale and release tension and notice the difference.
4. Concentrate on the difference between the two (tension-relaxation).
5. Tense muscles of mouth and jaw and release as above.
6. Progress through muscles of neck and shoulders.
7. Progress through the entire body: chest, stomach, arms, hips, thighs, calves, feet, and toes. Follow the same pattern of tensing and releasing, noticing the difference between these two states.

Meditation

Follow these simple steps:
1. Sit comfortably.
2. Reduce distractions.
3. Focus on your breath.

4. Just notice your breath going in and out. Notice your chest rise, belly expand, then collapse. Notice the temperature of your breath as it enters and exits your body.
5. Don't be discouraged by intrusive thoughts—let them wash over you.
6. When you find yourself distracted, simply acknowledge the distraction and return to focus on your breath.

Visualization

Follow these simple steps:

1. Picture a tranquil setting—real or imagined.
2. Imagine yourself in this setting.
3. Look around at the visual details.
4. Pay attention to specific smells, sounds, feelings, sensations.
5. Imagine how relaxed you can feel in this setting.

REFERENCES

American Psychiatric Association. (1980). *Diagnostic and statistical manual of mental disorders* (3rd ed.). Washington, DC: Author.

American Psychiatric Association. (1994). *Diagnostic and statistical manual of mental disorders* (4th ed.). Washington, DC: Author.

American Psychiatric Association. (2000). *Diagnostic and statistical manual of mental disorders* (4th ed., text rev.). Washington, DC: Author.

American Psychiatric Association (2013). *Diagnostic and statistical manual of mental disorders* (5th ed.). Arlington, VA: American Psychiatric Publishing.

APA Practice Guidelines. (2001). Practice guidelines for the treatment of patients with borderline personality disorder. *American Journal of Psychiatry, 158,* 1–52.

APA Practice Guidelines. (2004). Treatment of patients with acute stress disorder and posttraumatic stress disorder. Retrieved April 17, 2011, from http://www.psychiatryonline.com/pracGuide/pracGuideChapToc_11.aspx

APA Practice Guidelines. (2006). Treatment of patients with substance use disorders. Retrieved December 2013, from http://psychiatryonline.org/guidelines.aspx

Arnow, B. (2004). Relationships between childhood maltreatment, adult health and psychiatric outcomes, and medical utilization. *Journal of Clinical Psychiatry, 65,* 10–15.

Arnow, B. A., Hart, S., Hayward, C., Dea, R., & Taylor, C. B. (2000). Severity of child maltreatment, pain complaints and medical utilization among women. *Journal of Psychiatric Research, 34*(6), 413–421.

Arnow, B. A., Hart, S., Scott, C., Dea, R., O'Connell, L., & Taylor, C. B. (1999). Childhood sexual abuse, psychological distress, and medical use among women. *Psychosomatic Medicine, 61,* 762–770.

Back, S. E. (2010). Toward an improved model of treating co-occurring PTSD and substance use disorders. *American Journal of Psychiatry, 167,* 11–13.

Back, S. E., Killeen, T., Foa, E. B., Santa Ana, E. J., Gros, D. F., & Brady, K. T. (2012). Use of an integrated therapy with prolonged exposure to treat PTSD and comorbid alcohol dependence in an Iraq veteran. *American Journal of Psychiatry, 169,* 688–691.

Becker-Blease, K., & Freyd, J. J. (2006). Research participants telling the truth about their lives: The ethics of asking and not asking about abuse. *American Psychologist, 61,* 218–226.

Bloom, S. L. (1995). The germ theory of trauma: The impossibility of ethical neutrality. In B. H. Stamm (Ed.), *Secondary traumatic stress: Self-care issues for clincians, researchers, and educators* (pp. 257–276). Lutherville, MD: Sidran Press.

Bloom, S. L., & Farragher, B. (2011). *Destroying sanctuary: The crisis in human service delivery systems.* New York: Oxford University Press.

Bloom, S. L., & Farragher, B. (2013). *Restoring sanctuary: A new operating system for trauma-informed systems of care.* New York: Oxford University Press.

Bowlby, J. (1988). *A secure base: Parent and child attachment and healthy human development.* New York: Basic Books.

Bremner, J. D., Southwick, S. M., Johnson, D. R., Yehuda, R., & Charney, D. (1993). Childhood physical abuse in combat-related posttraumatic stress disorder. *American Journal of Psychiatry, 150,* 235–239.

Bremner, J. D., Vermetten, E., & Lanius, R. A. (2010). Long-lasting effects of childhood abuse on neurobiology. In R. A. Lanius, E. Vermetten, & C. Pain (Eds.), *The impact of early life trauma on health and disease* (pp. 166–177). Cambridge: Cambridge University Press.

Breslau, N., Kessler, R. C., Chilcoat, H. D., Schultz, L. R., Davis, G. C., & Andreski, M. A. (1998). Trauma and posttraumatic stress disorder in the community: The 1996 Detroit area survey of trauma. *Archives of General Psychiatry, 55,* 626–632.

Briere, J. (1992). *Child abuse trauma: Theory and treatment of lasting effects.* Newbury Park, CA: Sage Publications.

Briere, J., & Scott, C. (2006). *Principles of trauma therapy: A guide to symptoms, evaluation, and treatment.* Thousand Oaks, CA: Sage Publications.

Briere, J., & Spinazzola, J. (2005). Phenomenology and psychological assessment of complex posttraumatic states. *Journal of Traumatic Stress, 18,* 401–412.

Burgess, A. W., & Holmstrom, L. L. (1974). Rape trauma syndrome. *American Journal of Psychiatry, 131,* 981–986.

Campbell, R., Wasco, S. M., Ahrens, C. E., Sefl, T., & Barnes, H. E. (2001). Preventing the "second rape": Rape survivors' experiences with community service providers. *Journal of Interpersonal Violence, 16*(12), 1239–1259.

Chu, J. A. (1998). *Rebuilding shattered lives: The responsible treatment of complex post-traumatic and dissociative disorders.* New York: John Wiley & Sons.

Classen, C. C., Palesh, O. G., & Aggarwal, R. (2005). Sexual revictimization: A review of the empirical literature. *Trauma, Violence, & Abuse, 6,* 103–129.

Cloitre, M., Garvert, D. W., Brewin, C. R., Bryant, R. A., & Maercker, A. (2013). Evidence for proposed ICD-11 PTSD and complex PTSD: A latent profile analysis. *European Journal of Psychotraumatology, 4,* 1–12.

Compton, W. M. (2007). Prevalence, correlates, disability and comborbidity of DSM-IV drug abuse and dependence in the United States: Results from the national epidemiologic survey on alcohol and related conditions. *Archives of General Psychiatry, 64,* 566–576.

Connors, R. (1996). Self-injury in trauma survivors: 2. Levels of clinical response. *American Journal of Orthopsychiatry, 66,* 207–216.

Courtois, C. (1988). *Healing the incest wound: Adult survivors in therapy.* New York: W. W. Norton.

Courtois, C. (2004). Complex trauma, complex reactions: Assessment and treatment. *Psychotherapy: Theory, Research, Practice, Training, 41,* 412–425.

Courtois, C. A., & Ford, J. D. (2013). *Treatment of complex trauma: A sequenced, relationship-based approach.* New York: Guilford Press.

Courtois, C. A., & Gold, S. N. (2009). The need for inclusion of psychological trauma in the professional curriculum: A call to action. *Psychological Trauma: Theory, Research, Practice, and Policy, 1*, 3–23.

Danielson, C. K., & Holmes, M. M. (2004). Adolescent sexual assault: An update of the literature. *Current Opinion in Obstetrics Gynecology, 16*(5), 383–389.

Davies, J. M., & Frawley, M. G. (1994). *Treating the adult survivor of childhood abuse: A psychoanalytic perspective.* New York: Basic Books.

Dearwater, S. R., Coben, J. H., Campbell, J. C., Nah, G., Glass, N., McLoughlin, E., & Bekemeier, B. (1998). Prevalence of intimate partner abuse in women treated at community hospital emergency departments. *Journal of the American Medical Association, 280*(5), 433–438.

Deykin, E. Y., Keane, T. M., Kaloupek, D., Fincke, G., Rothendler, J., Siegfried, M., & Creamer, K. (2001). Posttraumatic stress disorder and the use of health services. *Psychosomatic Medicine, 63*, 835–841.

DiClemente, C. C., & Prochaska, J. O. (1998). Toward a comprehensive, transtheoretical model of change: Stages of change and addictive behaviors. In W. R. Miller and N. Health (Eds.), *Treating Addictive Behaviors* (pp. 3–24). New York and London: Plenum Press.

Du Mont, J., & White, D. (2007). *The uses and impacts of medicolegal evidence in sexual assault: A global review.* Geneva: World Health Organization Press.

Fallot, R. D. (2008). Trauma-informed services: A protocol for change. Presentation at Community Connections: Conference on Co-Occurring Disorders, Long Beach, CA.

Family Violence Prevention Fund's Research Committee (2003). Review of the US Preventive Services Task Force draft recommendation and rationale statement on screening for family violence. Retrieved March 26, 2014, from http://www.futureswithoutviolence.org/userfiles/file/HealthCare/FullResponse.pdf

Felitti, V. J., & Anda, R. F. (2010). The relationship of Adverse Childhood Experiences to adult medical disease, psychiatric disorders, and sexual behavior: Implications for healthcare. In R. Lanius & E. Vermetten (Eds.), *The hidden epidemic: The impact of early life trauma on health and disease* (pp. 77–87). New York: Cambridge University Press.

Felitti, V. J., Anda, R. F., Nordenberg, D., Williamson, D. F., Spitz, A. M., Edwards, V., . . . Marks, J. S. (1998). Relationship of childhood abuse and household dysfunction to many of the leading causes of death in adults: The adverse childhood experiences (ACE) study. *American Journal of Preventive Medicine, 14*, 245–258.

Firsten, T. (1990). *An exploration of the role of physical and sexual abuse for psychiatrically institutionalized women.* Toronto: Ontario Women's Directorate.

Fraser, G. A. (2009). The use of synthetic cannabinoid in the management of treatment-resistant nightmares in posttraumatic stress disorder. *CNS Neuroscience and Therapeutics, 15*, 84–88.

Freeman, D. W. (2001). Trauma-informed services and case management. In M. Harris & R. D. Fallot (Eds.), *Using trauma theory to design service systems* (pp. 75–82). San Francisco: Jossey-Bass.

Frierson, R. L., Melikian, M., & Wadman, P. C. (2002). How to interview depressed patients and tailor treatment. *Postgraduate Medicine, 112*, 65–71.

Gold, S. (2000). *Not trauma alone: Therapy for child abuse survivors in family and social context.* New York: Routledge.

Harris, M., & Fallot, R. D. (2001a). A trauma-informed approach to screening and assessment. In M. Harris & R. D. Fallot (Eds.), *Using trauma theory to design service systems* (pp. 23–31). San Francisco: Jossey-Bass.

Harris, M., & Fallot, R. D. (2001b). Envisioning a trauma-informed service system: A vital paradigm shift. In M. Harris & R. D. Fallot (Eds.), *Using trauma theory to design service systems* (pp. 3–22). San Francisco: Jossey-Bass.

Haskell, L. (2001). *Bridging responses: A front-line worker's guide to supporting women who have post-traumatic stress.* Toronto: CAMH Publications.

Haskell, L. (2003). *First state trauma treatment: A guide for mental health professionals working with women.* Toronto: Centre for Addiction and Mental Health.

Herman, J. (1992). *Trauma and recovery: The aftermath of violence: From domestic to political terror.* New York: Basic Books.

Hetrick, S. E., Purcell, R., Garner, B., & Parslow, R. (2010). Combined pharmacotherapy and psychological therapies for post traumatic stress disorder (PTSD). *Cochrane Database of Systematic Reviews, 7*(7), 2–4.

Janoff-Bulman, R. (1992). *Shattered assumptions: Towards a new psychology of trauma.* New York: Free Press.

Kahan, M., & Wilson, L. (Eds.). (2001). *Managing alcohol, tobacco, and other drug problems: A pocket guide for physicians and nurses.* Toronto, Ontario: Centre for Addiction and Mental Health, University of Toronto.

Karpman, S. B. (1968). Fairy tales and script drama analysis. *Transactional Analysis Bulletin, 7,* 39–43.

Kessler, R. C., Chiu, W. T., Demler, O., & Walters, E. E. (2005). Prevalence, severity, and comorbidity of 12-month DSM-IV disorders in the national comorbidity survey replication. *Archives of General Psychiatry, 62,* 617–627.

Kessler, R. C., Sonnega, A., Bromet, E., Hughes, M., & Nelson, C. B. (1995). Posttraumatic stress disorder in the national comorbidity survey. *Archives of General Psychiatry, 52,* 1048–1060.

Klerman, G. L., Weissman, M. M., Rounsaville, B. J., & Chevron, E. S. (1984). *Interpersonal psychotherapy of depression.* Northvale, NJ: Jason Aronson.

Klonsky, E. D. (2007). The functions of deliberate self-injury: A review of the evidence. *Clinical Psychology Review, 27,* 226–239.

Klonsky, E. D., Turkheimer, E., & Oltmanns, T. F. (2003). Deliberate self-harm in a nonclinical population: Prevalence and psychological correlates. *American Journal of Psychiatry, 160,* 1501–1508.

Kraemer, G. W. (1985). Effects of differences in early social experiences on primate neurobiological-behavioral development. In M. Reite & T. M. Fields (Eds.), *The psychobiology of attachment and separation* (pp. 135–161). Orlando, FL: Academic Press.

Lamprecht, F., & Sack, M. (2002). Posttraumatic stress disorder revisited. *Psychosomatic Medicine, 64,* 222–237.

Larkin, H., & Park, J. (2012). Adverse childhood experiences (ACE), service use, and service helpfulness among people experiencing homelessness. *Journal of Contemporary Social Services, 93*(2), 85–93.

LeDoux, J. (1996). *The emotional brain: The mysterious underpinnings of emotional life.* New York: Simon & Schuster.

Leichsenring, F., & Leibing, E. (2007). Supportive-expressive psychotherapy: An update. *Current Psychiatric Reviews, 3*(1), 57–64.

Levine, P., & Frederick, A. (1997). *Walking the tiger: Healing trauma.* Berkeley, CA: North Atlantic Books.

Lindley, S. E., Carlson, F. B., & Hill, K. (2007). A randomized, double-blind, placebo-controlled trial of augmentation topiramate for chronic combat-related posttraumatic stress disorder. *Journal of Clinical Psychopharmacology, 28,* 677–681.

MacLean, P. D. (1973). A triune concept of the brain and behavior. In T. J. Boag & D. Campbell (Eds.), *The Hincks Memorial Lectures* (pp. 6–66). Toronto: University of Toronto Press.

MacMillan, H. L., Fleming, J. E., Trocme, N., Boyle, M. H., Wong, M., Racine, Y. A., . . . Offord, D. R. (1997). Prevalence of child physical and sexual abuse in the community: Results from the Ontario health supplement. *Journal of the American Medical Association, 2,* 131–135.

MacQuarrie, B. (2007). *Implementing a woman abuse screening protocol: Facilitating connections between mental health, addictions and woman abuse.* London, ON: Women's Mental Health and Addictions Action Research Coalition.

Mason, R., & Schwartz, B. (2014). Responding to domestic violence in clinical settings. Retrieved July 5, 2014, from http://dveducation.ca/dvcs/index.php

McCann, I. L., & Pearlman, L. A. (1990). *Psychological trauma and the adult survivor: Theory, therapy, and transformation.* Philadelphia: Brunner-Routledge.

McCauley, J., Kern, D. E., Kolodner, K., Dill, L., Schroeder, A. F., DeChant, H. K., . . . Bass, E. B. (1997). Clinical characteristics of women with a history of childhood abuse: Unhealed wounds. *Journal of the American Medical Association, 277*(17), 1362–1368.

McColl, H., Higson-Smith, C., Gjerding, S., Omar, M. H., Rahman, B. A., Hamed, M., . . . Awad, Z. (2010). Rehabilitation of torture survivors in five countries: Common themes and challenges. *International Journal of Mental Health Systems, 4*(16).

Miller, W. R., & Rollnick, S. (2002). *Motivational interviewing: Preparing people for change.* New York: Guildford Press.

Miller, W. R., & Rollnick, S. (2012). *Motivational interviewing: Helping people change* (3rd ed.). New York: Guildford Press.

Mills, K. L., Teesson, M., Back, S. E., Brady, K. T., Baker, A. L., Hopwood, S., . . . Ewer, P. L. (2012). Integrated exposure-based therapy for co-occurring posttraumatic stress disorder and substance dependence: A randomized controlled trial. *JAMA, 308*(7), 690–699.

Najavits, L. (2002). *Seeking safety: A treatment manual for PTSD and substance abuse.* New York: Guildford Press.

Neumann, D. A., & Gamble, S. J. (1995). Issues in the professional development of psychotherapists: Countertransference and vicarious traumatization in the new trauma therapist. *Psychotherapy, 32,* 341–347.

Neumann, D. A., Houskamp, B. M., Pollock, V. E., & Briere, J. (1996). The long-term sequelae of childhood sexual abuse in women: A meta-analytic review. *Child Maltreatment, 1,* 6–16.

Newman, J. D., & Harris, J. C. (2009). The scientific contributions of Paul D. MacLean (1913–2007). *Journal of Nervous and Mental Disease, 197,* 3–5.

Newman, M. G., Clayton, L., Zuellig, A., Cashman, L., Arnow, B., Dea, R., & Taylor, C. B. (2000). The relationship of childhood sexual abuse and depression with somatic symptoms and medical utilization. *Psychological Medicine, 30*(5), 1063–1077.

Ogden, P., Minton, K., & Pain, C. (2006). *Trauma and the body: A sensorimotor approach to psychotherapy.* New York: Norton & Company.

Pelcovitz, D., van der Kolk, B. A., Roth, S., Mandel, F., Kaplan, S., & Resick, P. (1997). Development of a criteria set and a structured interview for disorders of extreme stress (SIDES). *Journal of Traumatic Stress, 10,* 3–16.

Porges, S. W. (2011). *The polyvagal theory: Neurophysiological foundations of emotions, attachment, communication and self-regulation.* New York: Norton & Company.

Pribor, E. F., Yutzy, S. H., Dean, T., & Wetzel, R. D. (1993). Briquet's syndrome, dissociation, and abuse. *American Journal of Psychiatry, 150,* 1507–1511.

Prochaska, J. O., DiClemente, C. C., & Norcross, J. C. (1992). In search of how people change: Applications to addictive behavior. *American Psychologist, 47,* 1102–1104.

Raskind, M. A., Peskind, E. R., Kanter, E. D., Petrie, E. C., Radant, A., Thompson, C. E., . . . McFall, M. M. (2003). Reduction of nightmares and other PTSD symptoms in combat veterans by prazosin: A placebo-controlled study. *American Journal of Psychiatry, 160*(2), 371–373.

Ravindran, L. N., & Stein, M. B. (2009a). Anxiety disorders: Somatic treatment. In B. J. Sadock, V. A. Sadock, & P. Ruiz (Eds.), *Kaplan and Sadock's comprehensive textbook of psychiatry* (9th ed., pp. 236–272). Philadelphia, PA: Lippincott, William & Wilkins.

Ravindran, L. N., & Stein, M. B. (2009b). Pharmacotherapy of PTSD: Premises, principles and priorities. *Brain Research, 1293,* 24–39.

Regier, D. A., Myers, J. K., Kramer, M., Robins, L. N., Blazer, D. G., Hough, R. L., . . . Locke, B. Z. (1984). The NIMH epidemiologic catchment area program: Historical context, major objectives, and study populations. *Archives of General Psychiatry, 41*(10), 934–941.

Saakvitne, K. W., Gamble, S., Pearlman, L. A., & Lev, B. T. (2000). *Risking connection: A training curriculum for working with survivors of childhood abuse.* Baltimore: Sidran Press.

Saakvitne, K. W., & Pearlman, L. A. (1996). *Transforming the pain: A workbook on vicarious traumatization.* New York: W. W. Norton & Company.

Scaer, R. C. (2001). The neurophysiology of dissociation and chronic disease. *Applied Psychophysiology and Biofeedback, 26,* 73–91.

Schachter, C. L., Stalker, C. A., Teram, E., Lasiuk, G. C., & Danilkewich, A. (2009). *Handbook on sensitive practice for health care practitioners: Lessons from adult survivors of childhood sexual abuse.* Ottawa, ON: National Clearinghouse on Family Violence.

Seedat, S., Stein, M. B., & Forde, D. R. (2005). Association between physical partner violence, posttraumatic stress, childhood trauma, and suicide attempts in a community sample of women. *Violence and Victims, 20,* 87–98.

Shea, S. C. (2002). *The practical art of suicide assessment: A guide for mental health professionals and substance abuse counselors.* Hoboken, NJ: John Wiley & Sons.

Siegel, D. (1999). *The developing mind.* New York: Guilford Press.

Spiegel, D., & Palesh, O. (2008). Trauma dans l'enfance et desire de vivre a l'age adulte: Trauma in childhood and risk for suicide throughout life. *Revue Francophone du Stress et du Trauma, 8,* 197–204.

Steele, K., & van der Hart, O. (2009). Treating dissociation. In C. A. Courtois & J. D. Ford (Eds.), *Treating complex traumatic stress disorders: An evidence-based guide* (pp. 145–165). New York: Guildford.

Stein, D. J., Ipser, J. C., & Seedat, S. (2006). Pharmacotherapy for post traumatic stress disorder (PTSD). *Cochrane Database Syst Rev, 1*(1), 8–15.

Sullivan, J. T., Sykora, K., Schneiderman, J., Naranjo, C. A., & Sellers, E. M. (1989). Assessment of alcohol withdrawal: The revised clinical institute withdrawal assessment for alcohol scale (CIWA-Ar). *British Journal of Addiction, 84*(11), 1353–1357.

Symonds, M. (1975). Victims of violence: Psychological effects and after effects. *American Journal of Psychoanalysis, 35,* 19–26.

Tavara, L. (2006). Sexual violence. *Best Practice and Research Clinical Obstetrics and Gynaecology, 20*(3), 395–408.

Tjaden, P., & Thoennes, N. (1998). *Prevalence, incidence and consequences of violence against women survey.* Washington, DC: National Institute of Justice & Centers for Disease Control & Prevention.

Ullman, S. E. (2007). Asking research participants about trauma and abuse. *American Psychologist, 62,* 329–330.

Ullman, S. E., & Filipas, H. H. (2001). Predictors of PTSD symptom severity and social reactions in sexual assault victims. *Journal of Traumatic Stress, 14,* 369–389.

US Department of Justice. (2003). *2003 national crime victimization survey.* Washington, DC: Office of Justice Programs, Bureau of Justice Statistics.

Vaillancourt, M. A., & Marshall, P. F. (1993). *Changing the landscape: Ending violence, achieving equality: Executive summary/national action plan.* Ottawa: Canadian Panel on Violence against Women.

van der Hart, O., & Dorahy, M. J. (2009). History of the concept of dissociation. In P. F. Dell & J. A. O'Neil (Eds.), *Dissociation and the dissociative disorders: DSM-V and beyond* (pp. 3–26). New York: Routledge.

van der Hart, O., Nijenhuis, E. R. S., & Steele, K. (2006). *The haunted self: Structural dissociation and the treatment of chronic traumatization.* New York: W. W. Norton & Company.

van der Kolk, B. A. (1987). *Psychological trauma.* Washington, DC: American Psychiatric Press.

van der Kolk, B. A. (1994). The body keeps the score: Memory and the evolving psychobiology of post traumatic stress. *Harvard Review of Psychiatry, 1*(5), 253–265.

van der Kolk, B. A. (1996). The complexity of adaptation to trauma: Self-regulation, stimulus discrimination, and characterological development. In B. A. van der Kolk, A. C. McFarlane, & L. Weisaeth (Eds.), *Traumatic stress: The effects of overwhelming experience on mind, body, and society* (pp. 182–213). New York: Guildford Press.

van der Kolk, B. A. (2005). Developmental trauma disorder: Toward a rational diagnosis for children with complex trauma histories. *Psychiatric Annals, 35*(5), 401–408.

van der Kolk, B. A., & D'Andrea, W. (2010). Towards a developmental trauma disorder diagnosis for childhood interpersonal trauma. In R. Lanius, E. Vermetten, & C. Pain (Eds.), *The impact of early life trauma on health and disease: The hidden epidemic* (pp. 57–68). Cambridge: Cambridge University Press.

van der Kolk, B. A., & Fisler, R. (1994). Childhood abuse and neglect and loss of self regulation. *Bulletin of the Menninger Clinic, 58,* 145–168.

van der Kolk, B. A., McFarlane, A. C., & van der Hart, O. (1996). A general approach to treatment of posttraumatic stress disorder. In B. A. van der Kolk, A. C. McFarlane, & L. Weisaeth (Eds.), *Traumatic stress: The effects of overwhelming stress on mind, body, and society.* New York: Guilford Press.

van der Kolk, B. A., Perry, C., & Herman, J. L. (1991). Childhood origins of self-destructive behavior. *American Journal of Psychiatry, 148,* 1665–1671.

van der Kolk, B. A., Roth, S., Pelcovitz, D., & Mandel, F. (1993). *Complex PTSD: Results of the PTSD field trial for DSM-IV.* Washington, DC: American Psychiatric Association.

Walker, L. E. (1977/1978). Battered women and learned helplessness. *Victimology, 2*(3-sup-4), 525–534.

Walsh, B. (2007). Clinical assessment of self-injury: A practical guide. *Journal of Clinical Psychology: In Session, 63,* 1057–1068.

Weissman, M. M., Markowitz, J. C., & Klerman, G. L., (2000). *Comprehensive guide to interpersonal psychotherapy.* New York: Basic Books.

Welch, J., & Mason, F. (2007). Rape and sexual assault. *British Medical Journal, 334*(7604), 1154–1158.

Widom, C. S., Czaja, S. J., & Dutton, M. A. (2008). Childhood victimization and lifetime revictimization. *Child Abuse and Neglect, 32*(8), 785–796.

Wolitzky-Taylor, K. B., Ruggiero, K. J., Danielson, C. K., Resnick, H. S., Hanson, R. F., Smith, D. W., . . . Kilpatrick, D. G. (2008). Prevalence and correlates of dating violence in a national sample of adolescents. *Journal of the American Academy of Child Adolescent Psychiatry, 17*(7), 755–762.

World Health Organization (WHO). (2013). *Responding to intimate partner violence and sexual violence against women: WHO clinical and policy guidelines.* Geneva: WHO Press.

Yatham, L. N., Kennedy, S. H., Schaffer, A., Parikh, S. V., Beaulieu, S., O'Donovan, C., . . . & Kapczinski, F. (2009). Canadian Network for Mood and Anxiety Treatments (CANMAT) and International Society for Bipolar Disorders (ISBD) collaborative update of CANMAT guidelines for the management of patients with bipolar disorder: Update 2009. *Bipolar Disorders, 11*(3), 225–255.

Yehuda, R., & McFarlane, A. C. (1995). Conflict between current knowledge about posttraumatic stress disorder and its original conceptual basis. *American Journal of Psychiatry, 152,* 1705–1713.

INDEX

abstinence models 93–6
abuse: in childhood 5–6, 8, 19, 25, 26, 28, 29, 56, 68, 75; children at risk for 43; chronic 21, 75, 121, 146; dynamics of 52; emotional 8, 23; fear/expectation of 32; history of 41–1; physical 5, 8, 19, 23, 82; prolonged 19; sexual 5, 19, 23, 29, 36, 68, 80; shame regarding 50; of women 60–2; *see also* domestic violence; substance use and abuse; trauma
abusive relationships: dynamics of 31–4; idealization of abuser in 8, 19; impact of 30–1
acamprosate 99
action stage 95–6; see also stages of change
acute stress disorder (ASD) 11–12, 15–16; diagnostic criteria for 140–1; in DSM-IV 15; in DSM-5, 15–16; history of, 15
addiction disorders: therapies adapted for use with 101; therapies developed for 100–1
adjustment disorders 12
Adverse Childhood Experiences (ACE) Study 29
affect 19;affect and dissociation 17, 18, 25, 104; dysregulation of 25, 31, 47, 82, 95; functioning 24–5; impact of affect dysregulation 47;-regulation of 25, 26, 56; regulation impairment 19, 21; self capacity 24; use of substances to modulate affect 83, 95
aggression 107–8

Alcoholics Anonymous 93
alcohol intoxication 88
alcohol use and abuse 49, 61, 62, 84; alcoholism 29; measurement of intake 85; *see also* alcohol intoxication; alcohol withdrawal; substance use and abuse
alcohol withdrawal 86, 88; complicated 97–8; uncomplicated 96–7
alkaline phosphatase tests 92
alprazolam 110
ALT 92
amitriptyline 111
amnesia 25, 68, 75, 91; anterograde 110; *see also* dissociative amnesia
amphetamines 85; intoxication 89; testing for 92; withdrawal 89
amygdala 65
analgesic medications 99
anemia 92
anger 14, 21, 32, 59, 62, 70, 107, 132, 138
anger control 107
anhedonia 89
antabuse 99
antidepressant medications 103, 107, 110, 111
antidiarrheal medications 99
anti-epileptic medication 97
antinauseant medications 99
antipsychotic medications 97, 106, 107, 110, 117–18
anxiety 8, 21, 24; symptoms of 107; *see also* anxiety disorders